EASY TARGET

Taming the Black Dog

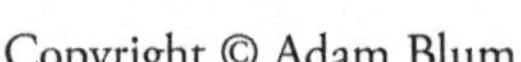

First published 2024

Big Sky Publishing Pty Ltd
PO Box 303, Newport, NSW 2106, Australia
Phone: 1300 364 611
Fax: (61 2) 9918 2396
Email: info@bigskypublishing.com.au
Web: www.bigskypublishing.com.au

Cover design and typesetting: Think Productions

A catalogue record for this book is available from the National Library of Australia

Title: Easy Target. Taming the Black Dog
ISBN: 978-1-923004-82-5

EASY TARGET

Taming the Black Dog

www.bigskypublishing.com.au

ADAM BLUM

ENDORSEMENTS

'This book is a must-read for anyone who thinks that "nasty words" whether written or spoken don't leave a lasting legacy. When those words are critical, mean and constant, the damage can run deep, and affect a person's life in ways that are unimaginable. But this isn't a sad tale that will leave you feeling flat … It is a powerful story of someone who faced all those demons and came out on top. I have no doubt Adam's honesty, courage, openness and journey of self-help, self-discovery and healing will assist others who are struggling with their mental health. He has shared his darkest moments and explained the constructive and helpful steps he took to regain control of his life. Bravo, Adam.'
Johanna Griggs, TV Presenter and Beyond Blue Director

'A truly inspiring tale of one man's struggles to overcome life's pitfalls. Adam's story is full of heart-wrenching and at times, hilarious reflections which leave the reader feeling there is always a way forward, no matter how tough the road. Be prepared to laugh, cry and take life by the horns!'
Amelia Adams, *60 Minutes* Reporter

'If someone had given me a book like this when I was a budding young man, I don't think I would have felt as lost and

alone all those years. A must-read to nurture perspective and understanding of those around us and especially ourselves. '
Paul de Gelder, Author, Veteran, TV Presenter and International Speaker

'If you were to look up the words "courage" and "inspiration" in the dictionary, there should be the name Adam Blum included in the definition. His is such a powerful story, told with such honesty and surprising humour for all that he has faced and endured. It's a tough story but also uplifting. I have no doubt that by sharing his story, Adam will help others overcome adversity. Well done on a ripper book.'
Deborah Knight, 2GB Sydney Radio Host / A Current Affair Host

'Adam's open and honest account of the difficulties life can present and his journey to defeating them is inspirational to say the least.'
Damien Thomlinson, Former Commando Motivational Speaker and Author

'This is a deeply inspiring book that touches the heart and uplifts the spirit. Adam Blum's story of fortitude, determination and courage to overcome challenges is a beacon of hope for those facing their own battles. Through sharing his journey, Adam reminds us that we are not alone in our struggles and there is always strength to be found within ourselves. Hilarious and honest. Heart-breaking and uplifting. This book is a testament to the transformative power of resilience …
Janine Garner, Author and International Speaker

'By being open, honest and vulnerable, Adam demonstrates immense courage in sharing his story. Adam has endured significant hardship throughout his life, yet his resilience in the face of adversity is incredibly inspiring. I have no doubt *Easy Target* will leave a lasting impression on all those who read it. The world is definitely a better place with Adam in it.'
Hugo Toovey, Army Major, Cancer Survivor and Founder of 25 STAY ALIVE

'Adam's story is a story of triumph in the face of overwhelming adversity at multiple stages in his life. Having overcome so much at such a young age, his story is a must-read for those suffering in silence on how to be inspired to turn their life around.'
Chris May, Veteran, Firefighter and Host of the *Dad Ready Podcast*

'Honest, kind and intelligent. These are words I already knew described Adam Blum. But strong, resilient and brave are what I have learnt about him since reading his book *Easy Target*. Told with unflinching honesty, this book shows Adam's true strength that has defied the bullies' taunts and the teacher who told him he would "amount to nothing". Instead, he has thrived because of them. Adam's book is a must-read for anyone who is struggling. It's an important story that will save your life.'
Donna Bourke, Former Warrant Officer Class 2 Army Intelligence and Author

'Adam displays the very essence of courage and vulnerability. This book takes us on a raw and authentic journey through his life's struggles and triumphs. We feel his pain and relish in his joy through his captivating narrative. Adam is a role model for young men in our communities and I have no doubt will save lives through his relatable *rose that grew from concrete* journey. It is an honour to call him a friend and colleague.'

Sarah Spicer, Qualified Firefighter, Fire + Rescue NSW

Easy Target is empowering on so many levels. Adam's raw candour throughout the book around his struggles are relatable, revealing that in the darkest moments of his life, he was able to find light. This book gives the reader the opportunity to imagine life beyond suicide and realistic ways to deal with years of thoughtless and at times unconscious behaviour from individuals. Absolutely inspiring.

Casey Nixon, Veteran and Mental Health Ambassador

ABOUT THE AUTHOR

Adam Blum had a troubled start in life. Born in 1992, he was plagued by debilitating health issues, and as an infant and throughout his childhood, endured a series of surgical procedures.

His school years were a torture. Experiencing both health issues and ADHD, Adam faced constant bullying. His self-esteem was shattered under the weight of the relentless taunts and physical abuse of his peers. The persistent bullying continued into adulthood and in the workplace. At the age of 22, and suffering from severe depression, Adam decided to take his own life. One phone call changed his destiny. Adam is still here to tell his story of the obstacles he overcame, of forging fortitude, and how, essentially, his life was twice saved while battling the black dog of depression.

Adam lives in the foothills of the Blue Mountains and is currently a firefighter with the NSW Rural Fire Service (RFS). He is the creator and host of a highly successful podcast called *True Blue Conversations Podcast* (formerly *True Blue History Podcast*). Adam hopes that the stories within *Easy Target* will help others build their own inner strength and self-worth.

Dedication

This book is dedicated to my late Nanna Robyn, the lady who inspired me to be all I can be in life. To my mum, Mandy, my dad, Ian, and my brother, Scott, I can't tell you enough how much your love and support has meant to me over the years and to this day. Thank you also to all my friends who have encouraged me throughout this journey; this is only the beginning of great things to come.

This book is also dedicated to my late great friend and brother, originally 4RAR Commando now 2nd Commando Regiment Warrant Officer Class 2, Nick Hill. Ride free, brother, till Valhalla. Rest in peace.

Warning for Readers

This book contains references to suicide, attempted suicide and suicidal ideation.

CONTENTS

FOREWORD

I got a direct message from Adam Blum asking me if I wanted to be a guest on his podcast about Australian veterans. I was busy, so I thanked him and deferred the invitation for six months and went back to work. At precisely the six-month mark, Adam appeared at my doorstop with a big grin, two microphones and a recording deck in hand. Adam had flown into Melbourne, hired a car, and driven an hour to see me. We sat in my home office and talked for an hour about life, transitioning from the military, and resilience.

During our conversation, I came to this conclusion about Adam and what drives him: he is a smart, strong and decent man who does great things in the name of helping others. Not only that, he embodies the one skill that can change everything: the willingness to transform and reinvent himself, no matter the pain or the difficulty.

Adam has faced his own challenges in life: limitations, injuries, disabilities and bitter disappointment. And yet, here he is: firefighter, podcaster, author and inspiration to many. A living example that from the ashes of tragedy, you can rise again, and be better for it.

I warmed to his good heart, and I hope in these pages, you warm to him too.

MARK WALES,
Author *(Survivor: My Life in the SAS)*,
TV Personality and Motivational Speaker

It was an honour to meet SAS veteran Mark Wales in 2022.

PREFACE

The Day Everything Changed

It was a cold day on 14 September 2014. I remember that the sky was blue and clear.

I was 22 years old and working in the construction/ earthmoving industry. While most guys my age were full of bravado, chasing girls and having lots of fun, I was not. Right from day one at school, I had been bullied. Bullied for pretty much everything. Bullied for merely existing. And it hadn't stopped when I entered the workforce.

My boss at the time didn't like me and to say I wasn't a fan of him either is an understatement! He used to ride me like I was a recruit at army basic training and he was my instructor. He was one of those hard, old-school blokes for whom nothing was ever good enough no matter how hard you tried to please him.

I had reached a point in my life where I believed everything that people were saying about me. I believed I wasn't good enough. When the boss turned up on the site where I was working that day, I knew I was in for a bollocking.

'Blum, you, bludger!' I looked up at him as he stormed towards me as I was shovelling the kerb. 'You're a liar, a thief and a waste of space!' he spluttered with saliva-covered lips.

You might think, *Adam, it's all good, people get yelled at by their boss all the time, shake it off.* But what you need to understand is that I was already in a very dark place – a place one should never enter – and I had been living in it for many years. The place was called Depressionville, population me. The boss's words were enough to push me even further into the depths of this murky city and literally to the edge of despair.

I finished work, and as I got into my car, I decided that I was going to end my life. I told myself that the world would be a better place without me in it.

I was oddly calm as I drove my white Toyota Hilux towards the cliff that would end me. I was completely at peace with my decision. But then I heard a voice …

INTRODUCTION
From Easy Target to Resilient Warrior

'You are so stupid, Blum!' the kid in my class yelled out so everyone could hear. The other kids laughed. The teacher told everyone to hush, but I could see behind his eyes that he agreed with the bully …

Learning has never come easily, and it still doesn't. To be honest, nothing comes easily to me; this means I must work for everything twice as hard, and that is not a bad thing. It has taken me a while to learn, but now I know that this shit just forges fortitude and character.

I was born at the Katoomba hospital on 5 December 1992. Dad was a linesman for Telstra and Mum was a community nurse in palliative care. I deeply admire my mother; it takes an incredibly special kind of person with heart and patience to be in such a role. She is caring, humble, my rock and one of my biggest supporters. One of the driving factors in my life is to make both my parents proud of me, and I strive to achieve this every day.

My first years of life were tough. When I was three months old, Mum and Dad found out that I had been born with only one teste; the second teste just never grew. For years this caused me great embarrassment. I felt different to others and wondered why I had been born this way. As I got older, this difference started to cause me mental distress and I would try to avoid going to the toilet in front of my peers. Many years later, I would learn that having one teste was not particularly bad.

At the tender age of nine months old, my parents faced another challenge. Out of nowhere, my seemingly normal eyes suddenly turned inwards, making me cross-eyed. Mum and Dad raced me to the doctors, who, given my presentation, initially thought I may have a brain tumour. Thankfully, tests showed that it wasn't. The doctors discovered that the muscles behind my eyes were very weak. An operation to tighten up those weak muscles was a success, only when I am extremely tired will my eyes start to turn inwards. With further surgery for an umbilical hernia and three sets of grommets, the first two years of my life were really difficult for my family.

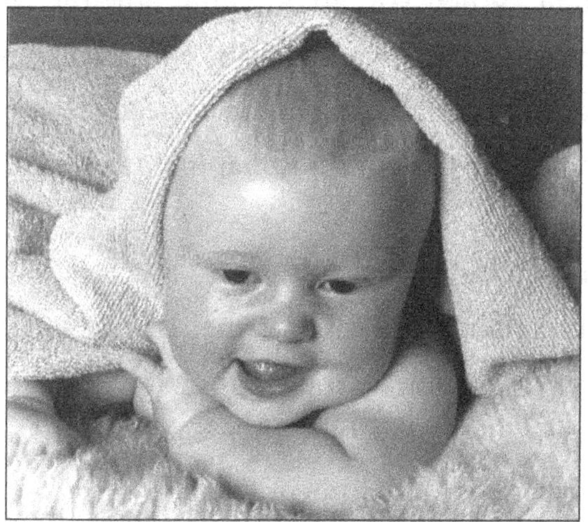

I was just six months old in this photo.

A target for bullies

'Here, catch this, fatty!' the boy said as he hurled the ball at speed straight at me. I quickly ducked, the ball just missing my head.

'Ha ha,' the boy laughed, 'Fatty can't even catch a ball!'

At school it became obvious that I was having trouble keeping up with most of the other students. At six years old (still in my first year of school), I was diagnosed with attention deficient hyperactivity disorder (ADHD) with learning difficulties. My older brother, Scott, was also diagnosed with ADD and learning difficulties. We were a handful, and we really didn't make it easy for our parents, who were already working hard just to make ends meet. Now they had two boys who both needed extra help, and that extra help cost extra money. In a typically Australian way, and in the way of their generation, they just put their heads down and bums up and got on with it. They did what needed to be done for both of us.

Being diagnosed with ADHD at such an early age did mean I could be treated appropriately, but it also confirmed to me that I was different. When you are a young boy, the last thing you want is to be different. I wanted to be able to read without long pauses, I wanted to be able to get the correct answer quickly, and I wanted to just have friends and happily play without a care in the world.

What we want and what our reality is can be quite different, and this was certainly the case for me. I struggled with literacy, I couldn't spell for shit and half the time everything on the blackboard was just a big blur that made no sense. Instead of laughing with friends, I had people laughing at me, pointing at me and calling me names.

My coordination skills sucked. Scott had also been diagnosed with learning difficulties, but he had been blessed with good hand-eye coordination and excelled at physical activities. I, on the other hand, was developing a body that was built for comfort not speed.

By the age of eight, I was already considered overweight. As if I didn't have enough going on with my body, I now had to contend with being a 'fatty' and as a little boy, there appeared to be nothing I could do about this.

Even though I was young, I had big feelings and emotions running around inside me. I could see that other children didn't appear to have these worries and thoughts that I had, and so I began to see my first counsellor. I knew people thought there was nothing wrong with my mental health and that I was just 'attention seeking'. I found myself worrying about what other people's thoughts were, and it stopped me from doing things for myself. I wish that I had kept up the professional help, but I didn't. I ended up just closing off and letting the hatred build up inside of me, not knowing what to do with all the pain that I was experiencing.

I hated that I was bullied, I hated the bullies, I hated the teachers, I hated that I struggled to learn, I hated that I wasn't good at sports, I hated my body and I hated that I had red hair and freckled skin.

Even though I had some amazing people in my life (people you will soon read about) I also had several toxic people who influenced me. In sixth grade one of my teachers told me that I would amount to nothing. Can you believe that? A teacher! He was in such an influential role and an authority figure, so I believed him and thought, *How can anyone who has disabilities like me get anywhere in life?* The kids at primary school and high school only ever brought me down. And I had a neighbour who told me that I would end up in jail.

I was an easy target. You didn't have to be a trained sniper to take the shot.

I was an easy target because I had not yet built up any resilience; I had no shield. I had no armour, but I gave everyone else ammunition to use. In fact, I was feeding the belt into the machine gun that they were firing at me.

Learning to blacksmith

Learning resilience and forging fortitude in the fires of adversity have been two of the biggest factors in me undertaking the un-fucking of my life. These lessons are not learnt overnight; it takes years to be trained as a blacksmith – to forge your own armour and create weapons and shields to protect yourself. I had to learn how to not be the target, how to deflect if I was spotted and zeroed in on, and what to do with the pain if I was hit.

What people do with the pain they experience can make a dramatic difference in the way they live their life. You can try to ignore the pain in the hope it will heal itself and just go away, but in doing so, the pain often just keeps growing quietly inside of you. Like a cancer that festers and eats away bits of you; in the end, it gets the better of you.

On the other hand, you can recognise the pain, understand that pain is a completely normal human feeling and add it to your armoury. It can be used to help build your resilience shield so you can encounter things in life and be able to deal with them in a rational way.

I did not have a resilience shield until very recently; I didn't even have an umbrella for protection. I was soaked in years of painful words and actions that had fallen on me and when my former boss's harsh words rained down on me that fateful day, enough was enough.

It never should have come to that point, but I had let it. Because I had learning difficulties, I genuinely believed that everyone was much smarter than me and therefore they were always right. If they said I was dumb, I was dumb. If they said I was a liar, then I was a liar. If they said I couldn't do it, then I couldn't do it. It has taken the past nine years to slowly get my head around the fact that they were wrong. I have finally accepted that just because someone has more book smarts than me does not mean every single thing they say is the gospel truth. I have learnt that I don't have to listen at all and more importantly, I don't have to care. I really don't have to give a fuck.

Realising that life sometimes sucks arse and that pain is a normal and a common part of it played a huge part in the process of building resilience and forging the sword of fortitude within myself. For example, an athlete does not stop running a race because they have a small blister. The blister is bloody painful, but the athlete understands that the blister is there and that it's common for a runner and so they just keep on running. The athlete doesn't suddenly stop feeling the pain of a blister – they are not a miracle worker – but what they have developed is mental resilience. This has been built by encountering many previous blisters. They understand the situation and what needs to be done for themselves at that moment; and what needs to be done is that they need to finish the race.

Battling depression

This book is titled *Easy Target* because until a few years ago I was a walking, talking target for people's nastiness, and the years of bullying and dealing with medical issues had given me low self-esteem and a poor, 'why me?' attitude. I have experienced the deepest, darkest bouts of depression, and I almost became a statistic; another one added to the long list of people who took their own life at a young age.

Over 65,000 Australians make a suicide attempt each year.

In 2019, 3318 Australians took their own life. Suicide is the third leading cause of death for Australians between the ages of 15 and 49.[1]

There are so many people of all ages and all walks of life who are battling an inner black dog. Although I'm only 31 years of age, I have been battling with my own head and health since birth, but over the past nine years, I have discovered that it doesn't matter how sucky your life may be, it can be un-sucked and it can be un-fucked. As I write this, I can tell you that my life is far from perfect. There are plenty of mornings that I don't want to get up and go for that run or swim – bed seems like the much better option – but one thing I have learnt on my journey is that the easy option is not usually the better one. I still have weight to lose. I don't have a wife or a girlfriend – hell, I don't even have a cat! But what I do have now is the will to live; a desire to come into my excellence and

1 Australian Government Department of Health & Aged Care, 2019, *Suicide in Australia*, viewed 4 January 2023, https://www.health.gov.au/topics/mental-health-and-suicide-prevention/suicide-in-australia.

a gratefulness for all the things that I do have, which I now realise, is so much.

Why I wrote this book

The old Adam died that cold winter's day in 2014, but Adam version 2.0 was born. I didn't know at 4 am when I got up to leave for work that it was the day when my life would change forever, the day when I would start my long and painful journey back from the depths of depression. It has been worth it, because it's this journey that has led me to un-fuck my life and write this book.

Easy Target is my story about overcoming adversity. When I started focusing on me, and what I needed to do for myself, everything changed. I started to become strong and not be such an easy target. I want to reach out to others who need help and share my journey. I'm telling my story because I will do what I can to make a difference. Even if it's just one person, that's one life saved and that's everything to me. I have also included some other people's inspiring stories of their life experience, their building of resilience and their own messages of hope and change.

Read on to find out how a phone call saved my life, and how a series of life-changing events, support from my family, developing resilience and forging fortitude, and finding my tribe brought me back from the brink, so that I am no longer a victim and I am no longer an easy target.

1
The Tiger Within

'Are you trying to kill that man?'

My grandmother looked up innocently at the senior nurse who had just walked in on her and the trainee nurse who was administering food to a patient.

'Why, no, sister. Of course not. I'm just giving him something to eat.'

'Cease it immediately. The patient is having his appendix out and is not meant to eat anything!' the senior nurse firmly instructed my grandmother.

So, it is no surprise that my grandmother did as instructed; however, what may surprise you is that my nan ended up marrying that patient. The guy she almost killed was my grandfather, Pop.

Robyn Stanton is my grandmother's name, the lady I know as 'Nan', and the lady who inspired me to write this book. I know that's a big call, but she impacted the first 12 years of my life in a way that only a nanna ever could.

Like many people growing up in her era, Nan didn't have an easy childhood. Life was hard for Australians at that time.

Australia had been involved in a world war, then a world depression, then just when things were picking up, there was another world war. Growing up in these times made people tough and some people just plain hard, such as my great grandparents. Nan was never shown any love as a child. I vividly recall her telling me about how when her baby brother was sleeping, her parents would put a pillow over her face to make her quieter so she wouldn't wake the baby.

Having such unloving parents could have made my nan into a downright bitch, but she turned out to be the complete opposite! She was compassionate and caring. At 17 years of age, she decided to get away from the toxic environment of her family home and put her caring side to good use.

Nan and Pop were married for 50 years and in 1958 they gave birth to my mother, who was blessed with the same caring and compassionate traits as Nan and who also chose work in the field of nursing.

In my childhood world of health issues, learning difficulties, physical differences and constant bullying, Nan was a shining beacon of hope and love to me. I loved how we would just sit at her kitchen table and she would tell me tales of her younger days, what it was like growing up in Australia and how things were for her as a young adult. I feel that this fuelled my interest in Australian history; an interest I have now pursued in the form of creating and hosting the successful podcast *True Blue Conversations Podcast.*

Nan taught me so many things. We built gardens together and did arts and crafts. She showed me that even though you may go through some horrible things, that doesn't mean you have to be a horrible person. She was patient, kind and intelligent. She listened to me when I told her how I was being bullied at school and I remember her words clearly:

> 'Adam, you are not stupid. You are my special boy. You learn things slower than others do and that's OK.
>
> **You have been put on this earth to achieve greatness and whatever you put your mind to you will achieve. You just have to believe that anything is possible.'**

***

In 1995 Nan was awarded the Premier's Award for her service to the community, including volunteering to cook dinners for the homeless and being on the Cancer Council. It was her service and selflessness that instilled in me community values; giving back is very important to me and is why I now serve with the Rural Fire Service of NSW.

One of the main reasons I never wanted to take up smoking was because when I was growing up, I saw Nan on oxygen and almost suffocating with every breath she took. Nan, who had earlier survived breast cancer, had developed emphysema and it was slowly killing her. I was only 12 years old, but I knew I had to savour every moment I had with the lady who meant so much to me.

The last trip I had with Nan before she died was a trip to Windsor, NSW. Windsor is a very charming and historic town on the outer regions of Sydney. Mum was there also, and it was a fantastic day. By that stage, Nan didn't get out much, and she was so happy to just be outside and somewhere different. We had lunch at an old cafe, and we poked around looking through the shops, where I spotted a tiger soft toy on a shelf. I boldly asked Nan if she would buy it for me and to my delight, she did! I still have that tiger with me today and it is with no shame that I tell you that it sits pride of place on my bed. When I'm feeling low, I look at the toy and remember that Nan really believed in me. It helps me to find the strength that is the inner tiger that stealthily resides within all of us.

The night before Nan passed away, I had a massive argument with my father. I wanted to go see Nan in hospital, but he didn't want me to see her in that state. Even though I was only a child, I swore at him, calling him every name under the sun. A few hours later, my father entered the room of the pubescent, seething, moody pre-teen that was me. He said to me, 'Come on then, I'll take you to see Nan.'

'Fuck off!' I yelled, throwing my stuffed tiger across the room at him. 'I'm not going with you.'

Well, not having a driver's licence and with little knowledge of the Sydney public transport system, I finally decided that if I wanted to see Nan, I needed to go with my father.

I sat down next to Nan at her hospital bed and she took my hand and squeezed it. She then removed her mask and spoke: 'It's beaten me this time.'

While Pop and the nurse were saying things like, 'No, don't be silly. You'll get through this,' I knew it was her time. It was her way of saying goodbye.

Nan's passing was very hard, she meant the whole world to me. That's why I cherish that faded and well-loved tiger on my bed. I look at it and I still see Nan. Nan, the lady who helped develop the tiger within me.

I was five years old when this photo was taken with Nanna Stanton.
She inspired me to write *Easy Target.*

2
A Mumma's Boy

I really was a little shit growing up. I was selfish and at times plain mean to my mother. I was so awful that I often made her cry.

I didn't mean to be such a shit. I didn't like seeing my mum cry. I knew firsthand what it was like for others to be mean to you because at the time, I was encountering that kind of behaviour every day. School was a living hell for me and I guess the only way I could vent was to take out all my anger and frustration on my parents.

Why am I like this? I would often think. My health problems, physical differences and learning difficulties often led to me pointing the finger at my parents. *It's all your fault,* I thought, referring to my parents. *You made me like this.*

The seething Adam was also a selfish creature. I wanted everything my way and if I didn't get it, all hell broke loose. In hindsight, I believe that at the time, I truly thought they owed me.

'Sorry, Mum, for making you cry and calling you names,' the note read. Despite often pushing Mum's buttons, the other thing

that I did know how to do was say sorry. After every big fight I would write Mum a sorry note. Mum still has in her possession every single sorry note that I wrote to her and I'm not proud to say, she collected quite a number over those years.

A mother's love for her son can never be broken.

Well, so they say, but I had a damn good go at trying to break it, then trying to fix it and then trying to break it again. Little did I understand and truly know back then just how caring, loving and utterly devoted my mother was to me and my brother, Scott.

'Your sons are going to end up in jail,' said our old grumpy World War II veteran neighbour to Mum.

Mum just huffed and walked away. Though my behaviour was at times appalling, it was hearing words like this spoken to my mother that made me want to be a better person and son. I wanted to make my parents proud, but it was easier said than done.

Nothing came easy to me and to be honest, nothing still comes easy to me now. I have had to work extremely hard to achieve anything, but this is all part of my journey. It is the way things are for me. I have learnt that

this is not something to be spiteful about but quite the opposite: it is something to be thankful for.

I am extremely thankful to my mother for all the sacrifices she made for my brother and me. We were these little fucks running around, wanting the world to revolve around us with absolutely no regard for our mother's own wants and needs. Mum's world was raising two difficult boys, being a supportive wife, working long hours in an extremely demanding job and defending her family at all costs.

I know both Mum and Dad's parenting skills were judged. It's easy for others to hand out criticism when they are on the outer and have no idea of the actual situation. What a shitshow it must have been for my parents to have two young boys both with learning difficulties and other medical issues.

Many well-intentioned people tried to give my parents advice and told them that they should not medicate us, but Mum and Dad made their own decisions about their sons' health and wellbeing. I now understand this would have been a tough decision and one they both did not take lightly. I am so grateful to them for following their gut instinct and choosing to medicate Scott and me. The medication meant that we could concentrate better in the classroom and have a chance at an education. I know some adults who had similar disabilities as children, but were not given the support that Scott and I received. Those guys ended up in jail. It's so important for struggling children to have support and have the right decisions made for them early in their life.

Not long ago I asked my mother, 'Do you have any regrets in the way you raised us?'

To my surprise she answered, 'Yes.'

'Go on,' I urged, interested in her reasoning.

'I wished I had spent more time with you guys when you were little, instead of going back to work so early.'

Because money was tight back then, Scott and I were put into care at a young age so Mum could get back into nursing and bring an income into the household. I had never held it against her, but she felt that if she had been around more when we were younger, then maybe she could have been able to make more of an impact on us and maybe we wouldn't have been such little shits.

Mum was a nurse for 44 years. Her long-standing service is a true testament to her character. Just like her mother (my nan), Mum's giving and loving nature is an inspiration for me. It is why I am telling this story.

I kept my suicide attempt (which I talk about in Chapter 9) a secret from my parents for a long time. Even though Mum has steely resolve, I didn't want to bring her any more pain. She had seen so much pain and suffering in her life, particularly with her work, that I knew she didn't need any more. I also didn't want her to think that she had failed as a parent, because God knows, she had done and continues to do, a sterling job.

I do often wish that I had been able to be more open with my parents. Of course, they knew growing up that I was being bullied and learning was difficult, but as I got older, I got more and more closed off about my reality and all the thoughts and feelings I had running through my brain and body. They were oblivious to just how dark a place I really was in and that was purely due to my not sharing the truth with them. This inability to speak openly and have mature, adult conversations free of anger and blame was my own undoing. If only I had the balls to speak up then Mum would have listened. She would have really listened, and she could and would have helped me. She was a nurse for God's sake, it was her job to help people, but more so, she was my mother and she really loved me.

I didn't speak up, though; like so many others, I just didn't have the words. Was it pride? Was it not wanting to be a burden on my mother and on society in general? Was it just me thinking it might just all go away? I'm still not sure what it was, but I have an inkling it was all of the above.

When I asked Mum if she had any regrets, maybe she should have asked me if I had any. Naturally, my answer would have been, 'Yes.' My biggest regret was not speaking first and foremost to my own mum about just how well and truly fucked up I felt.

Even though I was in all kinds of trouble as a kid, as I matured and acknowledge the ultimate and unconditional love that my mother had for me, I became what people describe as a 'Mumma's Boy'. Yes, I am a Mumma's Boy and hell, I am proud to say it. She is my rock and there is absolutely nothing wrong with that.

'A mother's love doesn't make her son more dependent and timid; it actually makes him stronger and more independent.'
Cheri Fuller

Mum has played such a huge role in my un-fucking-my-life journey. It's like she gives me oxygen when I find it hard to breathe and trust me, I often find it hard to breathe especially when I'm on an exhaustive run. Did I mention I use a snorkel to swim laps in the pool? I am not kidding.

When I ring her and tell her how I almost collapsed on my runs or how I nearly drowned doing my morning laps in the pool, she says, 'I'm very proud of you, Adam, you are doing great!' and it's like I can almost hear her smile down the line, and I can't help but smile back.

With Mum at Scott's wedding in 2023.

Our family photo taken in 2005.

3
My Father's Patience

'You can't sit up in that tree all day, you know. At some point you will have to come down.'

I sat up high in the big old gum tree that lived in our backyard. I loved that tree and the way it provided a natural playground for my brother and me. It gave us sticks to play with and make pointy things out of and it provided us shade and shelter. And right now, the tree was my shelter. It was sheltering me from the fury of my father and his dreaded feather duster.

No, my father did not want to tickle me with it, he was going to use the handle of it like a cane across my butt cheeks. I had felt that feeling before several times, but this time I had got away before Dad could punish me for being a prick.

Oh, yeah, I was a prick alright. I often got up to no good just to piss my father off. Looking back, now I think it's possible that I may have been seeking his attention.

I longed for my dad to pay me more attention.

Dad, however, only had so much attention to give. You see, he also has ADHD (undiagnosed, as they didn't undertake such diagnoses when he was a boy), and to put it bluntly, he was old. When I say old, he was 45 years old when I was born and so by the time that I was ten, he was a 55-year-old man with little energy to spare because he worked very long hours to help provide for the family.

The little energy that Dad did have seemed to be sent my older brother Scott's way. Unlike me, Scott had been blessed with athletic prowess and he was an excellent runner. He was so good he represented NSW as a junior and ended up long distance running at a national level.

Scott's running consumed Dad's free time. Dad would take Scott everywhere he needed to go for training and competitions while I was left to hang out with Mum. As you know, I adore my mum, but I craved my father's love and attention. Sometimes, we would all go to Scott's running events as a family. I fucking hated getting dragged around the countryside to these extremely boring events. I wanted to do what Adam wanted to do, not watch my brother win medals I could never win.

And win them he did, and so he was showered with praise, admiration and love. I just sat in the back seat of the car playing my Game Boy, seething with self-hate and getting fatter.

'It's almost dark and we're having dinner,' my father yelled up at me from the ground below the tree I was curled up in.

I could smell dinner and it smelled good. It suddenly dawned on me that I really was going to have to come down from the tree; who was I to think that I could mysteriously turn into a possum?!

So, me, the wannabe possum boy, climbed down from the tree and walked into the house rather sheepishly. *Whack*! That was the sound of the handle of the feather duster across the back of my legs. Tears welled up in my eyes from the pain.

Now, I have zero issues with being disciplined by my parents. It is technically known as legal chastisement, and I needed it. I needed disciplining, otherwise the old digger neighbour's words about me ending up in jail may have become the truth.

Dad had most certainly been disciplined during his childhood. Hell, I think everyone was back then. It was just the done thing. Unfortunately, though, Dad wasn't just disciplined, he was not loved by his own father. My father's disciplining of me wasn't because he didn't love me, it was precisely because he did love me, even though back then I didn't realise it.

Pa was my father's father and Pa was tough. He was a World War II veteran who had served in Dutch New Guinea and his service had taken a toll on him physically, emotionally and mentally. He showed Dad no real love.

Dad was an excellent athlete and played both A-grade basketball and squash. He was also a very good long-distance runner, which is where Scott got it from. Despite Dad's obvious athletic talent, his father still made him feel as though he couldn't do anything right.

'You, boy, are useless and hopeless,' Pa would say to Dad.

Though Dad was called 'useless and hopeless', he never called me that. Dad could see that I wasn't athletic and that I just needed to find 'my thing'. I'm happy to say that I have found my thing; however, it certainly has been a long time in the making.

Despite my distinct lack of hand-eye coordination, I love the game of soccer and it's all thanks to Dad. When I was only four years old, Dad taught me how to play. We kicked the ball around the backyard and Dad would smile when I put the ball through our makeshift goals. Seeing Dad happy made me happy and yes, he was spending time with me. His time was precious, Lord knows he didn't have much of it, so these little father–son moments meant the world to me.

***

Boom, came the sound of the thunder. It sounded so close that I thought the house was going to lift from the ground and we wouldn't be in Kansas anymore. My brother and I sprang out of our own beds and raced down the hall, entering Mum and Dad's room with speed and hopping in to the safety of their bed. Mum cuddled Scott, assuring him the storm would pass. Dad held me tight. I remember his strong arms wrapped around me; his hug made me feel that I was safe and, most importantly, that I was loved.

I don't know how much he loved me, though, when I was learning to drive. Dad had taken on the highly frustrating role of teaching his ADHD-with-learning-disabilities-with-complete-unco-ness 16-year-old son how to drive a manual vehicle.

Not surprisingly, a few years earlier, Scott had taken to driving like a duck to water. For me, on the other hand, driving was a completely different story. I have no idea why Dad let me drive Scott's ute, but he did. It was three weeks since I had first sat behind a steering wheel and for some reason, I was now learning in Scott's pride and joy.

Bang, came the sound of metal against the tree trunk. No, it wasn't my favourite tree in the backyard. This tree was out the front and I had reversed straight into it! Dad looked at me, shaking his head as he realised that I had hit the accelerator instead of the brake.

Not long after, both Dad and Scott sat down with me and told me a home truth. 'Adam, you are putting too much pressure on yourself. You are tense and anxious. Just relax, take your time and the driving will come more naturally.'

Though I was a defiant teenager, I actually listened for once to their advice and within a short time frame, my driving had dramatically improved. I'm proud to say that I successfully passed my driving test for my car licence and I went on to get my truck licence and bike licence … *broom-broom!*

Dad and I had a distant relationship, for want of a better word, but over the past few years as I have undertaken the journey of forging fortitude and finding myself, I have rebuilt a good relationship with my father. This rebuilding has come with me being able to look outside of my own little world and see the bigger picture. I can now see the man my father was and is. The man who had a hard childhood, the worker with his own undiagnosed ADHD, the loyal husband and the older father with only so much free time and energy.

Through his own actions, Dad has shown me what values and morals are and, importantly, what hard work is. He has shown me that

no one is perfect and no one is a perfect parent and that's OK

as long as you do the best you can. Dad has always done the best he can and now I am doing the best that I can. I want to thank my father for showing me these things and teaching me important life lessons while still loving me unconditionally despite my often testing and trying ways. I can only hope to develop the patience of that of my dad. Though my mum is more saint-like, my father does indeed have the patience of one.

With Dad at Gallipoli on Anzac Day, 2015.

4

Building a Brothers' Bond

I wanted to be Scott. I could never beat him at anything unless it was who could drink a can of Coke the fastest or piss off Dad first. For the longest time, I wanted to be my older brother.

Everything came easily to him. That's what I thought growing up, but little did I know that Scott had his own issues. He too had a disability (ADD) with learning difficulties like me. I did know that but it just didn't register how this may be affecting him, because as a young boy all I saw was how great he was at sport and how he was with his hands. He could build anything. Me, I struggled putting together my Lego set.

'Come on, Adam, in the car, we have got to get Scott to the race on time,' my father ordered me. I turned off the TV, grabbed my Game Boy and slowly dragged my feet down the hall, out of the house and into the back seat of the old family sedan.

'You got the grumps up?' Mum asked, noticing my mood as Dad drove the car down our street.

I didn't answer.

'You know, if you were a competitive runner, I'm sure Scott would come along to watch and support you, isn't that right, Scott?' Mum said, turning her head around from the front seat to look at Scott.

'Sure would,' Scott said with a big smile.

He wasn't lying. He would have supported me because he has always supported me. The truth is Scott is probably my biggest fan. He has shown unconditional love to me despite my medical issues, my self-loathing and my selfishness.

'Yeah, bro, you can do it!' Scott said to me as I looked at the dirt jump we had built in the bush. I, meanwhile, was certain it meant my near-death.

I looked at him as I straddled my BMX bike, trying to build up the courage to take on the jump. He smiled at me in an encouraging way and nodded his head. I closed my eyes and pushed off, pedalling as fast as I could before I hit the jump and opening my eyes as I was in the air. Suddenly, I was back on the earth, still on my bike and still alive.

I'm not sure why I was always such a chicken. I seemed to be afraid of everything, but Scott had no fear.

It has only been in the past few years that I have learnt to live with the fear and use it to my advantage.

Now, I fight fires and get winched out of helicopters. I'm still often scared as hell, but I do it anyway and I do it well.

'Make sure you are back before dark,' Mum would call out while standing in the driveway in her pink dressing gown for all the neighbours to see.

'Yes, Mum,' Scott and I would call back in unison as we rode our bikes away from the house and headed straight for the bush to build our dirt jumps.

Our jumps were built in the bush which was on council land. Technically we weren't supposed to be conducting our own earthworks on council property, but we never littered, and it wasn't hurting anyone apart from us and our mates when we came off our bikes and received the occasional bruise and graze.

Despite our best efforts to not piss anyone off with our bush builds, we still had to regularly move our jump sites after someone would complain to council about 'kids mucking around in the bush'. One day, though, we really did piss someone off. I'm not sure who had the brilliant idea of destroying the headwall of the drain outlet, but we did. A neighbour who saw what we had done appeared out of nowhere, resembling the local yowie. He was large and hairy and very, very scary. He told us abruptly we better tell our parents what we had done to council property before he rang the police. Scott and I hastily rode home and sheepishly informed Dad about our vandalism. Rather than giving us a bollocking straightaway, Dad went out and cleaned up our mess. On his return, Scott and I were both grounded for four weeks.

I certainly learnt my lesson about not destroying anything that is not your own!

***

I once noticed Mum poke her head up from a book she was reading. She was happy and tanned as she sat on a beach, book in hand, admiring her little Blum family unit. She smiled at me and I smiled back. She then quickly put her nose back into her Mills and Boon.

We were on our biannual family vacation at Coolangatta near the New South Wales/Queensland border. This event lasted for 14 whole days and it was the highlight of my life at the time. It was 14 days away from the bullies and the horrors of school. It was 14 days of sunshine, sand, saltwater and quality family time together.

For Mum and Dad, it was a much-needed vacation. They both worked so hard, and money was tight, but they always put away enough for us to have this traditional family getaway. Looking back, I don't even know how they did it. It must have cost a bomb for two weeks away with two hungry boys, but they always provided.

Because Dad worked so much, he seemed to be rarely home. However, Scott was always there and

Scott unintentionally stepped into the father role in my life.

Though he was only five years older than me, I looked up to him, always trying to imitate what he did even though we all know most of the time it was to no avail. Scott, with his talents and patience, did teach me quite a few things. Scott is a qualified tiler and now has his own successful tiling and bathroom renovation business. He taught me his trade of tiling; I learnt how to screed and mix up, how to use power tools and cart tiles.

During a ten-day trip to Fiji, Scott and I decided that we would buy a block of land together and build our own house on it, together.

'What? You guys are kidding yourself,' came out of the mouths of a few people when we got home from our South

Pacific trip and informed our families, friends and workmates of our plan.

I was suddenly down, as no one seemed to be excited for me and Scott and our plan for the future. 'Fuck them,' Scott said to me, seeing that my smile had been turned upside down. 'We are going to do it. You and me, bro. We can do anything together.'

And we did. In 2014 we bought a block in the suburb of Hazelbrook that backed on to some beautiful bushland. In 2017 we started the build. The build took eight months in total and with Scott's trade and building abilities and my eagerness to prove everyone wrong, we built ourselves a beautiful home, together as brothers, standing side by side.

I recently asked Scott what he thought about my gastric band surgery and weight loss journey (more on this in Chapter 16), as for some reason, I had never asked him that question before. 'Well, you were *hangry*. You know, angry because you were hungry, before your surgery when you had to drop some kilos. To put it bluntly, you were a prick.' Scott then continued, 'I was proud of you, though. I am, I'm real proud of you.' As I put the phone down, I could feel the tears start to well in my eyes. It was moving for me to hear Scott say he was proud of me.

Scott is now a father to a beautiful little girl, Matilda. I absolutely adore my niece and Scott is undeniably a great father. I can only hope that if one day I become a father I can be like Scott. Yes, I still want to be *like* Scott.

With Dad and Scott at the Hazelbrook Anzac Day Service, 2022.

5

The Freckle-Faced Fart Machine from Kmart

Among the large number of bullies I have encountered and still encounter (no, it hasn't stopped) this one boy stands out. I could type his name here, but I have learnt that acts like that don't earn you any respect. This brown-haired boy was 14 years old when he first graced my presence. He would set out to hurt me, and had an aura that made me want to run and hide. He hated all my 115-kilogram guts and I, in return, hated his.

There was no escape from his torment. No matter where I would go in the playground, he would sniff me out. He would find me in the quadrangle, he would find me on Cressy (our school sports field) and on the oval, and even if I made my way into the bush, he was there.

His favourite name for me was 'The Freckle-faced Fart Machine from Kmart'. The name made zero sense apart from the fact that, yes, I had freckles. I now realise it's such a ridiculous name to be called that it's actually very funny and makes for a good book chapter title.

'Hey, fathead, how'd you get so fat?' he would call out in a rhetorical fashion. Fathead was his other favourite name for me.

Just leave me alone, I thought to myself, wishing he would just disappear. He didn't disappear, though, he was always there. Like the bills and taxes adults had to pay, he was there and coming for me.

The bully knew what he was doing. He would always make sure I was alone when he would start his torment and he wouldn't finish until he could see that I was hurting. Though he didn't physically hurt me, he emotionally hurt me, and that is most certainly just as bad and probably even worse.

'Hey, freckle-faced fart machine from Kmart, you are the laughing stock of the whole school! You are so dumb!' I clearly remember him saying to me on the bus one day. Yes, the bully was on my bus. As I said, there was no escaping him.

That's not exactly true. There was one place where I found some reprieve and that was in the school library. The library was my one safe haven and place of refuge. I would bury my head in books that I struggled to read in order to just have some peace.

The hell continued all through high school too. I think it may have even got worse as I developed acne on top of my freckles. Now, the same bully's new name for me changed from 'fat head' to 'pimple face'.

All I ever wanted was to be left alone.

I just wanted to sit in the playground and eat my Vegemite sandwich in peace. Me and my red hair weren't causing anyone any trouble. My farts weren't that bad and my acne was my problem, not his. I didn't want to draw attention to myself, but apparently when you are overweight, have red hair, freckles, pimples and are a slow learner, you are like an injured gazelle to a pack of hungry lions.

I often asked myself, *Why can't they just leave me alone? They* being the bully plus others. The bully certainly wasn't alone in his crusade in making my life a living hell. It's a question that still has no rock-solid answer. Even through years of therapy, this question hasn't been answered. I mean, the psychologist will make suggestions along the lines of, 'People who bully have their own insecurities, so targeting someone they feel is lesser or weaker than them just makes them feel better about themselves.' This may be true, but maybe, just maybe, they are all just a bunch of cowards. Sick, sadistic people who get enjoyment out of seeing others suffer. Much like serial killers, really.

Bullies don't go to jail. Serial killers do, but not bullies. They should, though. They should be persecuted for their sick actions. Bullies undoubtedly take more lives (or screw them up) than serial killers do. In recent times, given the increase in workplace and cyber bullying, the authorities have tried to introduce some laws around bullying and there actually being some serious repercussions for the offenders. Nevertheless, it's still at an all-time high. You only just have to jump on any social media platform or chat group to see the disgusting behaviour of a huge number of sadistic people.

***

It was a bully who drove me to my attempted suicide. My former boss.

My former boss was the type of man who would say, 'You

know, it's a privilege for you to be working here for me,' like I was some loser he had employed off the streets.

It was as though you owed him a pound of flesh. I had to work six days a week regardless of other commitments on the weekend. Asking for a Saturday off was as impossible as getting blood out of a stone.

My wisdom teeth had come through and were causing me pain and so I needed to have them removed. The dental procedure was booked, and it required me having a few days off and I was absolutely petrified to ask for the time off. I remember walking up to him, quivering. 'What do you want?' he asked abruptly. With little confidence, I stated my request. My request wasn't denied; however, I could tell he was pissed off at one of his employees having to have a medical procedure that, Lord forbid, required a Saturday off from work.

Though my request for days off to have my dental procedure hadn't been denied, my request for another watercart to come help me, as I was working between five different job sites at the one time, was. His statement to me was simple and just downright bullying behaviour; 'Too bad. You are just going to have to work harder.'

In 2013 there were bushfires in NSW, and I wanted to do my part and go help with the bushfire effort, so I asked my boss.

'Adam, if you want to go fight fires you won't have a job. You must choose between fighting fires or working here.'

You piece of shit, I thought to myself, hoping that his own property caught alight and there would be no one there to save it. Now, I know that sounds harsh, but this really showed me the man's true colours and they all resembled shades of excrement.

Like at school, it wasn't just the one bully. When I told people at my workplace that I was going to start my own podcast, they made fun of me.

'Yeah, right, Blum, you're dreaming,' one of my colleagues said, laughing, as he bit into an apple during smoko.

I just sat there quietly thinking that maybe he was right, maybe I was dreaming. Starting up a podcast is not an easy feat despite every man and his dog seemingly having one these days. Competition is stiff and I knew nothing about broadcasting. What I did know about, though (and have a passion for), was military history and in particular Australian military history. Yes, I had learning difficulties, but my brain seemed to absorb facts about history like it was a sponge. I also had a huge yearning to help veterans' stories be told. I wanted to be the voice for their stories so they had a legacy. I wanted to hear and tell the stories not just of the semi-famous decorated soldiers but of the older diggers, the operators in roles that no one cared about but made the military work each day, and the female veterans who everyone had forgotten about. I knew this podcast needed to come to life.

I smiled back at the apple-eating workmate. 'We'll see.'

I've been teased about writing this book too. I know there are many people who are just laughing at me thinking, *WTF? How is he going to write a book?* I also know there's a little bit of jealousy happening too, now. Back in my younger years, the bullies certainly weren't jealous of me, but now, there is some jealously. There's jealousy because Scott and I built a beautiful home together at a young age when they're still living with their parents or renting. There's jealousy because I went to the 100th Anniversary of the Gallipoli Landing and since then have visited the Western Front on multiple occasions. There's jealousy because I have a job with the RFS where I winch out of helicopters, and there's jealousy because I made my dream of starting my own podcast come true.

In all honesty,

one thing I have learnt is that many people don't want to see you succeed.

Seeing others succeed makes them feel insecure or that they are not good enough. This is, of course, a pile of shit, but unfortunately that is how the human brain works. Fortunately, though, not everyone wants to see you fail. I have my tribe who continuously build me up (find out more about them and their stories in Chapter 27). They want to see me succeed and they help me every day to achieve my goals. This is because they are high achievers themselves. If you want to succeed, you need to be around those who want to see you succeed.

If there is a bully in your life, try to remove yourself from them because the chances of them realising they are not a nice person and should stop that type of behaviour is probably zero to none. Now, I am able to stand up for myself if I am faced with being bullied, but the fact is that this isn't going to change that person, it just means they will probably find an easier target than me.

Removing negative and toxic people from my life and surrounding myself with those who pull me up rather than bring me down has been one of the greatest things I have done to un-fuck my life. My tribe never bullies me. Rather, they make sure my head isn't big and my feet are firmly placed on the ground. Despite a number of them being spiritual, they are not off with the fairies, and they make sure I'm not tinkerbelling either. They pull me into line and give critical yet not condemning feedback. They let me know it's OK to not do everything at once, but to make sure I'm getting my now not-so-large arse out of bed and into the pool for some laps.

I know there will always be bullies in the world, some people are just built like that. But there's something I can do and there's something you can do. Try your best to be nice, even if a person is a freckle-faced fart machine from Kmart.

6
Gingers Have Souls Too

'You are the ugliest person I have ever seen,'

said the young, blonde woman to me as if I were a piece of dog shit stuck to her imitation designer stiletto.

'That's a bit harsh, don't you think? I know I ain't Brad Pitt and I may not be everyone's cup of tea, but the ugliest person you have ever seen? Really?' That's what I should have said in reply to that blonde, but no, I didn't have the confidence or even the ability to laugh at the absolute ridiculousness of her statement. I didn't even understand just how shallow a human being she was.

I was 20 at the time. These were supposed to be my prime years. I was allowed out to nightclubs and allowed to drink and have a good time with my mates and go out and meet girls, but now the girls I was meeting were just plain mean.

Mean girls, great … I thought. Just another demographic to add to the list of 'We are all out to get Adam'. My list was getting was very long.

I was lined up to buy a drink at the Lapstone Hotel when I heard her say that. I did spin around to see who was insulting me. The woman was laughing, making fun of my red hair, acne, double chin and all of my 120 kilograms. I turned back around to face the bar, ignoring the taunts from behind, but what she said couldn't be ignored. It was burnt into my brain and soul. She had said I was the ugliest person she had ever seen. Because she had said it, it must be true. I must be that ugly.

I never spoke of that night for many years. Even through hundreds of hours of therapy following my suicide attempt, I still never mentioned it. Not once.

Why not, Adam? Why not? you ask. I can hear you saying, *That's the type of shit that definitely needs talking about.* Well, it's only recently that I have realised that, and also how much this night affected me and caused my suicide attempt.

That one person, a shallow, stiletto-heeled blonde woman who was and still is a stranger to me, made me hate myself. She made me hate the way I looked. Her words cut me so deep, I feel the wound is only just starting to heal, now, ten years later. She made me feel like an absolute piece of shit. Worthless and that no one would want me. I used to think, *Why would anyone want to go out with me? Have sex with me? Marry me? Have a family with me? How could anyone want someone so ugly?*

During my journey of development and self-discovery, I am discovering a deeper understanding of the human condition.

I now understand shallowness.

I now realise that the mean girl was simply shallow and couldn't see past the outer shell of any person. She had no care or consideration for the human being residing inside. She was the ugly one. Ugly inside. The movie *Shallow Hal* springs to mind, doesn't it?

I know I'm not a ten out of ten. Now, even with clear skin, no double chin and 60 kilos lighter, I may not be 'art in motion', but I know I'm not Deadpool. I am somebody's cup of tea. I might sound like a wanker saying this, but inside I am a ten out of ten. I give myself a high rating in terms of how I treat others, how I care, how I give and how I love.

I have lots of love to give. I have a big heart and yes, I do wear my heart on my sleeve. I know that this is sometimes to my detriment; however, I am learning who to give my heart to.

'You know, Adam, your face is aesthetically pleasing. Everything is in proportion, and you have no outstanding features and that's a good thing …' my fashion model friend said to me, smiling.

'Ha, ha, no outstanding features … I like that,' I replied.

She laughed as she spoke: 'It's true. Your skin is clear, and you look good with a shaved head.'

Yep, now I have a shaved head, not by choice mind you and it's not to hide my red hair. It's to hide the fact I am losing my hair. That's correct: at only 31 years of age, I am balding.

The doctors have attributed my hair loss to me only having one teste. It just gets better! You know I'm being sarcastic, right? But that is the reason. Apparently, I produce a very high level of testosterone and the testosterone creates a layer in my scalp which then somehow causes the hair loss. Look, I could get all technical but I'm not going to; all I know is that my hair is falling out!

I didn't realise how much I appreciated my red hair until I didn't have it anymore. I was always teased about it, as is standard for most of us with this hair colour. If you make fun of someone's cultural background, you are labelled a racist. If you make fun of someone's sexuality, you are labelled homophobic, but you can call a redhead 'Fanta pants' and everyone thinks it's hilarious. Well,

Gingers have souls too.

Years of being called 'Ranga' broke my soul. Years of being bullied about my weight broke my soul. Being told I was 'useless and would never amount to nothing' by my sixth-grade teacher broke my soul, my former boss broke my soul and that shallow blonde broke my soul.

What is good, though, is that my soul is being put back together. I was a broken mess and an easy target, but now I am rebuilding myself into the real Adam, Adam 2.0. I am proof that the phoenix can rise from the ashes; you can improve your life by being patient with yourself and learning to love yourself, by getting the support you need to grow emotionally and by realising that growth will change your life.

7
A Few Good Friends

Hindsight is a funny thing. When I was young, I thought I had friends; even though I was bullied, I still thought I had a strong friendship circle. Turns out, I didn't have a circle. I can now see that I had more of an arc. I was an outsider. Those who I thought were my friends were for the most part just people who entered my space on a daily basis.

I did do my best to interact in a socially normal way, but having disabilities meant that my 'normal' wasn't everyone else's 'normal'. I've said it before and I will say it again, having red hair, being overweight and having other disabilities made me stick out like a sore thumb, and who wants a sore thumb? No one. No one except some very special people who could see past the sore thumb to the other working digits.

The Mountain Boys didn't mind a sore thumb; hell, I think they each had more than a sore thumb each day given our antics on our bikes. Kyle, Dylan and Ben. We were known as 'The Mountain Boys'. We became a brotherhood. A neighbourhood brotherhood that played street cricket and tried not to smash the old lady down the street's windows. We went on bush walks and talked about who could jump the highest on their bike. We did everything together and they have given me many fond childhood memories which I am very grateful for. It is easy to get caught up in all the shit I encountered as a child and teenager and so easy to forget the good times. The thing is, there were good times and Kyle, Dylan and Ben helped to create plenty of these good times. Twenty years later, we are still mates and catch up regularly. Yes, The Mountain Boys are still talking shit about who can jump the highest.

***

She walked into the room with a big egg on her head and an even bigger smile on her face. She had just come from a game of hockey straight to my friend's 13th birthday party displaying her egg head plus a doozie of a lump and bruise on her leg. I immediately thought she was great.

Her name was Jackie and her personality lit up the room and got the party started. Fortunately for me, Jackie and I hit it off straightaway and we became thick as thieves.

Jackie has seen me at my best, but she has often seen me at my worst. When the shit hit the fan, Jackie hung around despite the possibility of being hit by a piece of faeces.

'You know, Adam, you sharing your struggles has really helped me,' Jackie recently said to me.

'How so?' I asked, not really realising the depth of what she was saying to me.

'I've been having my own struggles, struggles with my mental health, but watching and listening to you, it's given me hope and a new level of understanding.'

Hearing one of my long-term friends tell me this really hit a chord. It reminded me that I was not the only one battling and that it wasn't all about me. Most people struggle at some point in their life and no matter how perfect someone's life may appear, all may not be what it seems to be.

***

Jackie played hockey, but Kristen played volleyball. That's where Kristen and I met, on the volleyball courts. I was in year ten and most girls were starting to look pretty good. Kristen did look good to this teenage boy's eyes, but like Jackie, it was her personality that I was drawn to.

Kristen is a paradox; she's one of the kindest and caring people I know, but at the same time she is fearless and ferocious. She actively pursues her goals, like a cat after a mouse, and one would rather step aside than get in her way.

'Blum, you are acting like a baby. Stop it,' Kristen told me when I was having a cry over spilt milk or something.

We all need a friend who doesn't hold back from telling you the truth. Most of us don't want to hear the truth, but sometimes, we need to hear it. Kristen is that friend.

'I was always so negative, but you never gave up on me,' I said to Kristen during a recent conversation.

She smiled. 'Blum, despite the negativity, I could see beneath that. I always knew you would find your way back to the light. Back to the light inside.'

***

Now, I can't talk about these amazing people I call friends without talking about Jamie. Jamie is 20 years my senior and when I was a young tacker, I used to wave at him as he drove past my house. Strangely, our paths would cross again over a decade later. It was in 2014 when Jamie joined the RFS and was stationed at my brigade. He, like myself, had a calling to serve and he wanted to help his community how he could. Jamie and I shared many common interests. Motorcycles are one of them and it was Jamie who showed me how my supposed 'brothers' in the motorcycle club weren't 'brothers' at all. I invited Jamie to a club ride and it was on this ride that Jamie saw what I had been blind to, their bitchiness and backstabbing. He was that angered by it that he even approached the club president and spoke to him about the members' behaviour. Jamie's insight plus a shift in my mindset helped me make my decision to leave what was a really toxic environment.

***

Good friends are like gold. Finding them is rare. They are precious and special. Despite all my shit, my friends have stuck by me, walked with me and in some cases, carried me. They have been amazing. One thing I have learnt, though, is that it cannot always be about me. It cannot always be about you. Any relationship is a balancing act. A fine balance of listening and talking, of laughing and loving, of acting and learning. I have learnt that I'm not the only one who has struggles and just as much as I need them, my friends also need me.

8
Falling in with the Wrong Crowd

I felt like my life was spiralling out of control. I truly felt I had no control over anything in my life and I had been sucked up into some tornado that was throwing around my emotions, my health, my finances, my cognitive abilities plus any ability to think rationally and see things for how and what they really were.

After I finished high school, I worked for an earthmoving company because I believed that was the only thing I would be capable of doing; digging and moving dirt. I was 21 when I got my real first job. I was so proud because there were people who told me I would never get any form of employment.

'This will show them,' I said to myself on my first day at the job.

As soon as I met the crew, I wanted to be just like them. I wanted to be one of the boys and laugh with them at their jokes. It didn't take long, however, for me to become the butt of their jokes. I would share my thoughts and goals with them and they would turn it into a joke at my expense. I would laugh along, not fully understanding that I was being bullied by the guys who I looked up to and was trying so hard to be like.

My neediness to be liked by them meant that I did something stupidly reckless at work, thinking it would impress them, but instead it got me fired. They thought I was an idiot and then I went and did an idiot thing right in front of them. I shake my head at myself now for being such a try-hard, but back then all I wanted was to be liked.

The phone call to my mother was hard.

'Mum, I've been sacked,' I said to her, tears in my eyes.

'Why? What happened?' she immediately asked.

'I did something stupid. I fucked up on the job. I feel like a failure,'

I sobbed to her.

After the phone call ended I sat in my car for 30 minutes, just frozen. I finally regained enough composure to drive back to my parents' house where I was living and to face the music.

My parents and grandparents had done their best to instill the right values in me from a young age, but now I was losing sight of all these values and lessons they'd taught me. I would have sold my soul to the devil to fit in. I wasn't fitting in, though, and my mental health was in a bad state of rapid decline. I just felt like a loser and I didn't want to feel like that anymore, so I went looking for something to numb the pain and make me feel a whole lot better …

Alcohol made me feel better. Hell, it made everything better. I started drinking all the time, hiding my drinking as best I could from my family and my friends. I guess they call it substance abuse. I would go out on the town and drink and drink until all the bullies, all the torment and all the self-loathing had been drowned by the bottle.

I felt happy and without a care; that was until the following morning when I would always wake up with a hangover and with the attitude of a grizzly bear that had been awoken from hibernation.

'What's wrong with you?' my dad would ask me as I made my way into the kitchen.

'Nothing. What's wrong with you?' I would snap back.

I was a volcano on the verge of erupting, all the time. I had no care or consideration for my words or how I was treating the people around me, those who actually cared about me.

I was now part of another crowd. A crowd that chased highs because of how low they were.

I was quickly becoming a product of the people I was associating with.

Surprise, surprise, the high was always temporary. Once I was sober again, I would slide further into the black dog's claws. Depression had a nasty grasp on me. When my family asked if I was OK, I replied that I was fine. I would then go out and get shitfaced, and my family never knew about the excessive drinking and partying.

It didn't take long before the alcohol wasn't enough to numb my pain, so I self-medicated with party drugs.

Now, I was experiencing a whole different kind of high. I felt unbelievable. I felt happy and, more importantly, I felt free. Carefree. I wanted more of that feeling and I chased that feeling. I began to crave that feeling.

Coming down was a whole other matter; it was a shit feeling, worse than you ever thought you could feel. I didn't have the maturity back then to seek professional help. I thought that self-medication was my only option and that I could deal with my own issues in my own way, even though deep down, I knew that my way was not the right way. I was going against all the values I had been taught. I was losing my sense of self.

I opened up and told my best friend that I was substance abusing. The look on her face was one of utter disgust. I think that's why I never told my family about what I was doing when I started trying to help myself. I was ashamed.

I was never going to write this chapter. This whole part of my story was going to remain a secret, as I didn't have the balls (ball) to face my mum and tell her what I had done. I spoke to a mentor of mine about the substance abuse and she said, 'Adam, you must put that in. It's an important part of your journey. Many people can and will relate.'

I shook my head at her. 'No, I can't. I cannot let my mum find out. She will be devastated.'

'Well, it's your book and it's your call,' she replied.

I stewed about this for many months and it wasn't until I had a deep conversation with a man who I highly respect that I decided I needed to bite the bullet and get these words down on paper.

It was only this morning that I rang my mother. 'Ads, how are you?' she asked, answering my call.

'I'm good, Mum, but I want to tell you about something.'

'What is it?' she asked in her loving tone.

'Well, I'm about to write another chapter for the book, but I need to tell you about it before I write it. I don't want you read it and find out that way. I need to tell you now.'

'OK, you can tell me.'

I hesitated. *Come on, you've got to tell her now. You've come this far.* 'Mum, when I was in my early twenties, after I lost my first job, I was in a bad place mentally. I didn't know what to do but all I know is that I wanted to just feel better so I started substance abusing.'

There was a pause down the line as Mum ruminated on my words.

I continued. 'Mum, I'm not proud of this. Far from it. I've been so ashamed because you brought me up better than that, but back then, I just wanted to numb the pain.'

As the tears welled up in my eyes, Mum's voice came down the line. 'Ads, you are my backbone. I turn to you and look to you for strength, all the time. I'm sorry you felt that you couldn't tell Dad and me.'

It was like a weight had been lifted off my shoulders. Finally, I have the monkey off my back. I had been carrying around that drunken, fucked-up monkey for nine years and now it is gone!

It took the suicide attempt to get myself out of the substance-inflamed tornado that I was living in. Following my suicide attempt I sought professional help and that professional help put me onto prescription medication to help level out my brain and emotions. Though I was most certainly not fixed, it was the beginning of the un-fucking of my life and doing something to help myself escape the black dog's hold.

I'm not proud of my past. But I am proud that I've had the courage to finally tell my parents about this time in my life and proud that I have been able to write about it and share it with you.

We all have our shit.

We have all made mistakes and done things that we are not proud of and now shake our heads at. This too is a part of the journey. I had to reach the lowest of lows before I could start climbing back towards the light into a brighter future.

9
The Cliff

Brrring... That was the sound of my alarm in my ears at 4 am that morning. I pulled my 160-kilogram arse out of bed and towards the bathroom in a daze. Little did I know as I stepped into the shower cubicle that in 12 hours' time I would be standing on the edge of the cliff and about to throw myself off ...

The day started like any other. I was now employed with another earthmoving company in a job I hated. The main reason I hated the job was the people. My work colleagues made fun of me and the boss was the worst person I had ever met. They say the devil wears Prada. Well, I say the devil wears hi-vis.

I drove the watercart and wetted up the road base ready for the grader, I then moved onto shovelling the gutters. I had worked hard all day, but at 3 pm, not long before knock-off time, my devil of a boss drove onto the job site in his fancy Mercedes 4WD. He parked his car and watched me from afar.

I was big, and it didn't take much for me to work up a sweat, but regardless of that, I was entitled to have a drink of water as needed, so I stopped for a moment, putting down my shovel and picking up my water bottle in its place. When he saw me doing this, the boss started up his Mercedes and drove over to me at lightning speed. He pulled up right in front of me, opened his driver's side door and started screaming at me before he had even made his way fully out of the vehicle.

'Blum, you're a liar and a thief,' he yelled at me. 'You're a bludger too. If I didn't give you this job you would have nothing.'

He carried on for a few minutes telling me how 'I owed him' and it was a 'privilege to work for him'.

The devil had been looking for a soul to destroy and he had found his target in me. I was a slow moving, easy target and the boss was the lion going in for the kill, breaking down its prey minute by minute, piece by piece until I was completely disembowelled.

It has taken many years of therapy and, I guess, maturity to understand why people chose me to pick on. Is it because the bullies always pick on the vulnerable target? Being overweight, having medical conditions, red hair, and no doubt an obvious lack of self-confidence meant I stood out like an injured gazelle. Bullies themselves are cowards and gutless, and that boss was the most gutless coward I have ever come across.

***

My soul had been broken many times in the past by a range of people, but this time I was rocked to the core. I had had enough. I was a broken man.

After the abuse, the devil drove off, leaving me to finish the shovelling. I worked until it was knock-off time then I gathered up my things and left the job site without saying goodbye to anyone.

I drove past the turn-off for my house, instead weaving my way up the hills into the Blue Mountains. Nothing played through the speakers of the ute's radio. All I had to listen to were my own thoughts. My thoughts believed everything the boss had said to me and they told me the best decision would be to end my life. That way, the pain would be gone. I wouldn't be a burden on society, on my family or on myself.

I believed that my family would be better off without me; I never really considered how much my killing myself would affect them. I never once thought that they would be devastated to lose their son, their brother or their nephew. I gave no thought to how my actions would impact their lives. I didn't think that me taking my own life would cause any mental anguish and related issues for those closest to me; that I would be putting them through years of pain and suffering. Not once did such thoughts enter my mind.

I have now learnt that there is a flow-on effect after a suicide. The life of one person may be over, but the lives of others go on and are never the same again.

The carpark I drove to was covered in mist, which made visibility low as I pulled up to those cold hills. The temperature had dropped dramatically and though the day had started out sunny and bright, the weather was now miserable. I suddenly didn't feel miserable. I felt at peace. I was more than comfortable with the decision to take my own life and with how I was going to do it. I was going to throw myself off the cliff's edge.

Probably due to the crappy weather, there was not a soul in site. This particular spot was often packed with bushwalkers and sightseers, but on this day, it was just me.

I walked towards the edge of the cliff, disregarding any rails or warning signs. As I stood there on the edge, the clouds parted, and a ray of sunlight shone down on me. I felt the warm sunlight on my face and as I was about to depart from this earth, I heard a voice. Now, some might say it was God speaking to me, but I know it was my nan.

'Adam,' said Nan, 'stop. Pick up your phone and make a call.'

I always listened to Nan and this time was no different. I stepped back from the cliff's edge, pulled my mobile phone out of my pocket and hit the phone number for the first person on my contacts list.

The person immediately answered. 'Blum Dog, how are you doing, mate?' The person's name was Mick, and he was a very good friend at the time. Mick and I are no longer close friends, but I have learnt that people come in and out of your life as you need them. Mick was there for me when I needed him most.

'Not good, mate. Not good at all …'

I sat there, amongst the mist and the evening air for four hours as I poured out my heart to Mick. He just listened, asking only the occasional question. Finally, when I was done with my tell-all, he said, 'You need to get help, mate, professional help. Where are you?'

I answered, 'I'm not telling you where I am, but I will go home, and I will get help.'

Mick paused then asked, 'You promise? You promise you will go get help?'

I answered yes and then we ended the call.

I often wonder if I would have jumped if Mick hadn't answered that call. I truly don't know the answer. All I do know is that he did answer, and that phone call saved my life.

I didn't go to work the next day, instead I went to the doctor.

Telling the doctor that I had just experienced a suicide attempt was extremely hard. I felt weak for speaking up about my mental problems. Of course, it was the opposite. I was strong for talking about it. It takes strength and courage to speak up, admit your issues and seek help.

Unsurprisingly, the results from my mental health assessment were off the charts, so the doctor immediately referred me to a specialist psychologist and prescribed antidepressant medication.

It took three years and several specialists before I found a psychologist who really got me and made me understand what the root of the problem was and who could provide some actual solutions.

I recently sat down with a friend of mine, a former Queensland Police veteran and told him my story. He asked me, 'Adam have you stopped and reflected on the journey to this point and how far you have come?'

I shook my head and answered, 'No, I haven't. I guess I've just kept moving forward, just kept myself busy.'

He looked at me with those eyes that have seen so much and said, 'Adam, you need to stop and reflect, brother. It's an important part of the process of working on your mental health.'

I have taken this man's advice and have started to do this, to take time for reflection. For example, the other day my coach, Sarah, said, 'OK, Adam, I want you to do a brick session where you go out on the bike for 20 kilometres and then straight off the bike and run for 10 minutes to simulate a triathlon.'

My first thought was, *Fuck that, I'm not up for that yet*, but I did it. Yes, it was tough, but I got it done, and as I was sitting on the lounge after the session (still thankful to have not had a cardiac arrest) I thought, *You know what? I'm going to create a reel for Instagram* and so I did! I used the images and video I captured on the day from the session and then added in some old photos of the former me at 162 kilograms. The reel showed me just how far I have come, and it was really more for me than for anyone else. As I looked at the old photos I was blown away and I thought, *I really have come such a long way from that day in 2014, 14 September, when I wanted to end it all.*

As I wrote this, I saw that another young military veteran and AFLW star killed herself on the weekend. She was 28 years old and had everything to live for but felt so overwhelmed that she couldn't go on anymore. It made me sad to think that she must have felt that there was no one there to help her through her struggles. It made me realise that my own mindset has completely changed. I no longer believe that there is no hope. I have worked for years to improve my life and put me in a positive mindset and develop rational thinking, maturity, resilience and fortitude. I have surrounded myself with inspirational people who are in my corner to help me if I start to fall. I have learnt there will still be times when you are not going so great, but getting through these tough times makes you stronger as a person. I stop and reflect on the journey, as it's not the end destination we look forward to, it's the growth along the way.

10
Saving Grace

'Dad, you know what?' I said to my father as we walked down the street following the 95th ANZAC Day service held in my suburb.

'No, what?' Dad asked as he looked at me proudly wearing my grandfather's World War II medals pinned neatly onto the right side of my chest.

'You and me, we're going to go to Gallipoli for the 100th anniversary of the Gallipoli landing,' I stated in a matter-of-fact tone.

Dad smiled as he spoke. 'Maybe, son, maybe.'

Ever since being presented with my grandfather's medals at the tender age of six, I had been interested in military history and in particular, Australian military history. Dad would always take Scott and me to the Anzac Day marches and I felt very proud and humbled to be able to wear Pa's medals. Little did I know that this would light a fire in my belly and lead me to achieve my goal of attending the 100th anniversary of the Anzacs at Gallipoli in Turkey standing alongside my father. And to create a path of being able to help tell veterans' stories through my own Australian military history podcast, originally titled *True Blue History Podcast.*

I knew the trip to Gallipoli was a big goal for a young man to set, but I also knew it was achievable. Of course, it was going to be very expensive, and Dad and I didn't have much money, but we did have some time, so we started to put money aside for the big adventure.

'Why does Australia have to be so fucking far away from everywhere?' I swore as I looked at the prices of international flights and how many hours I would be in the flying tin can. I shook my head, realising that travelling internationally for a major event was a logistical nightmare. Now there was also a danger factor to throw in too. There was talk of the Gallipoli anniversary possibly being the staging event for a terrorist attack, and the authorities had sent out warnings to those intending to travel to Turkey for the commemoration.

Mum was worried. 'I don't want anything to happen to you over there. You and your father mean too much to me. I don't know if you should go.'

I looked at Mum, holding her coffee mug with both hands as if it were a form of security. 'We are going, Mum; it's already paid for. Dad and I have been saving forever for this trip and it's important. It's important for us.'

I wasn't wrong about it being important for us. Only the year prior, I had attempted suicide. The suicide attempt had been extremely hard on my parents. My relationship with Dad was still strained, to say the least. This trip was about finding common ground, and it was something we both wanted to do together.

'I understand,' Mum said, taking a sip of her coffee. 'Your father is really looking forward to it. He's not looking forward to the plane trip, though …'

'Yeah, well, he will forget all about the plane trip once we are there. We are on the tour so there will be heaps of other people with us. It will be fun and safe,' I replied confidently.

I had managed to get us onto the Mat McLachlan Battlefield Tour, which provided the leading tour for the 100th Anzac Day anniversary to Gallipoli. Being part of the tour meant that most of the logistics were taken care of. It had been a big weight off my shoulders and I knew we would be in good hands and get to see all the sights that I longed to see.

***

The international flight to Istanbul was loud and full of people just like Dad and me – people headed over to Turkey to walk in the footsteps of the Anzacs. Excitement was in the air, and no one spoke of any possible terrorist attack. I had squeezed myself into my chair, just hoping I could get out when I needed to go to the toilet. Goodness knows I couldn't hold on for the whole 20-hour flight!

In Turkey, I was amazed by just how beautiful the country was. Everything about it was different to Australia. I hoped Dad was open to this very new cultural experience.

'I'm sorry, but you are not booked into this hotel for tonight,' the hotel receptionist said to me.

I looked at her like she must not know her job and said, 'Yes, we are. Please check again.'

The receptionist tapped on her computer then looked up and said, 'There are no reservations under your name.'

Dad was pissed off. Tired, hungry and in a foreign country, he snapped, 'What are we going to do now?'

'Don't worry, Dad, I will sort this out,' I said, trying to calm him down.

Dad didn't calm down. One thing about my father is that he does have a short temper. 'How can I not be worried? Here we are in a foreign country, we don't speak the language and we don't know anyone! I don't even know where I fucking am right now!' he exclaimed, referring to the hotel's address.

I thought I had better go talk to someone from McLachlan Tours. I found a staff member from the tour and told her the situation. Luckily for us, she was able to sort it out. You see, we were supposed to have booked the hotel for that night prior to the tour starting, but good ol' Mum, who I had assumed had booked it, hadn't.

At dinner that night, we met the rest of the tour group and visited the Hagia Sophia and the extraordinarily beautiful Blue Mosque, before all jumping on the bus to make our way to Gallipoli.

To put us all in the right mood, the 1981 film *Gallipoli* was playing on the scratchy TV that was on the coach. At the end of the movie, Dad looked at me and said, 'Adam, I can't believe I'm here with you. Thank you for making this happen.' I knew then that this was the start of us rebuilding our relationship.

***

'Fuck, it's cold,' I said as I stepped off the bus to head towards the Dawn Service.

'You're not wrong,' Dad replied as he did up his jacket. It was –4 degrees Celsius, but the wind was blowing straight off the water and it felt more like –20. I was about to start grumbling about the conditions again when I had some type of epiphany. I realised that here at Anzac Cove, 100 years ago, men my age and younger would have faced the same weather conditions, and that was the least of their worries … So, I never complained about the weather again on the trip.

The service was everything I expected it to be, and I felt so humbled to be there with Dad, sharing this unforgettable experience. With so many people in attendance, it took a few hours to get out of the service, back on the bus and undertake the bus ride back to the hotel. By the time I arrived to my room I was stuffed, but I still felt moved by Gallipoli and couldn't help but think about those young men charging the beach. I said to Dad, 'Let's just rest for 30 minutes, then we'll go down to get breakfast.'

Seven hours later we had missed breakfast and lunch and we were starving. We left the confines of our hotel in search of food. We roamed the streets looking for places to eat but couldn't find any. Looking back, I'm sure there were plenty of eateries, it's just that we didn't know what we were looking for. Like little lost boys, we wandered around sticking out like sore thumbs and looking rather dumb.

'I'm going back to the hotel. I'm not hungry anymore,' Dad said in a grumpy tone resembling a toddler.

'Don't be an idiot,' I replied. 'We need food.'

Finally, there it was. A sign we recognised. It shone like a shining beacon of hope. It was a Burger King.

'Yes!' I exclaimed, now almost so hungry my arm was starting to look good. I made my way towards the beacon of gastronomic satisfaction when I noticed Dad was not following me.

'What are you doing? Come on,' I gestured to my old man.

'I'm not hungry,' he said, folding his arms as a sign of his resolve.

I shook my head at his immature behaviour. 'Yes, you are,' I told him. 'Come on!'

I walked into the Burger King and my father begrudgingly followed. We then indulged in what was probably the best tasting Whopper Burgers we have ever had. Things between us improved after that.

The next few days were very emotional for me. I had the whole tour group come over to comfort me after they found me sobbing at the grave of a 22-year-old soldier. It had been so moving walking from Johnson's Jolly to Lone Pine. After signing the memorial book, Dad and I had a little spare time, so we wandered through the cemetery and it was there that I broke down.

You see, the universe has a weird way of working and it led me to stop at the grave of a 22-year-old soldier who was killed on 7 August 1915. This boy was only 22 when he lost his life. He didn't want to die, but he did, and I cried for him. Only the year before I had attempted to take my own life at 22. For the first time in my life since my suicide attempt, the word 'selfish' entered my mind. This young soldier had been so selfless in his service to his country, which ultimately took his life. Now I was thinking about how selfish my act would have been.

At that grave, Dad kneeled beside me and put his arm around my shoulders, comforting me. He said, 'Adam, you've come so far in the past year. I'm proud of you.'

That moment with Dad is one that I will never forget. The whole trip, I will never forget. Like the dates on the tombstones, it is etched into my mind. So many lives were lost at Gallipoli, but mine was saved. Though I had technically already saved my life, this trip breathed new life into me and made me realise just how precious my life really was and it was not to be taken for granted. It also saved my relationship with my father. Gallipoli was my saving grace.

11
Go West

'You know, my great-grandfather served on the Western Front,' I said proudly to Karen from Mat McLachlan Battlefield Tours while on tour with them in Gallipoli.

Karen smiled and replied, 'Well, then, you should come on one of our Western Front tours.'

My love of military history, in particular, Australian military history, all started when I started researching my own family history. Military service played a large part in my family history and the more I researched it, the more interested I became. However, it was not until 2015 that the fire was well and truly lit inside my belly.

In 2015, I had taken Karen up on her offer and visited the Western Front for the very first time.

I was able to stand on the ground where my relative was killed, and this stirred something inside of me that I could not shake.

Walking the ground where 46,000 men fell was such a moving and emotional experience for me. It's one thing to read about it in books and watch documentaries, but it's a whole other experience to walk the ground where the Anzacs fought and died.

This first tour of the Western Front lasted four days. I visited Pozieres in France, where there had been 23,000 Australian casualties over a duration of six weeks of intense fighting. The famous quote from Charles Bean, Australia's official war historian, best sums it up: 'The Pozieres ridge was more densely sown with Australian sacrifice than any other place on earth.'

The men there were simply slaughtered, as if they'd entered some ghastly giant mincing machine. It really tells you about the reality of the fighting and what the Anzacs faced as they went into that battle. My great-great uncle fell in the first day of the battle and is buried at Gordon Dump Cemetery. As I stood at his grave I thought about how he went to a war 12,000 miles away for the grand adventure, unaware of the horrors that he was going to face, and he was only 22 years old, the same age I was when I had my suicide attempt. Standing at his grave was something I will never forget as it was truly a very moving experience.

As part of the tour, we visited the town of Ypres, now known as 'Ieper' in Belgium. This is where the fighting centre was and hosts the flat fields of Flanders and the scenes of mud and blood which have been captured in many artworks. The town itself was totally destroyed in the fighting.

The Last Post Ceremony has been held every night at the Menin Gate every year since 1928 (except for the occupation of the Germans in World War II). The gate was completed in 1927 and records the names of the 54,000 men who went missing and as such have no known graves. As I stood there on that cool night when I attended, the Last Post gave me goosebumps, and made the hairs stand up on the back of my neck.

I explored the famous battlefields where the Anzacs fought – Hill 60, the Menin Road, Polygon Wood – and then visited Tyne Cot cemetery, where 12,000 Commonwealth soldiers are buried. It was there that the true cost of war really hit me. The most moving site that I visited was Fromelles, where 5533 casualties were sustained in 24 hours of fighting. It is still Australia's single worst military disaster. Standing on that flat open ground, I imagined how awful the battlefield would have been for the soldiers, with the dead, dying and the wounded all around them. I just couldn't imagine how scared these men would have been and how brave they were.

The Cobbers Memorial Sculpture of Sergeant Fraser carrying a wounded soldier over his shoulder is a reminder of the mateship between these men. It is a mateship that is instilled in not just the Australian military but Australian society. The code states that you stand up for your mate and you never leave a mate behind. These blokes weren't fighting for King and Country, they were fighting for their mates who were fighting right there beside them. We all have mates who we would do anything for; it is what the Anzac legend is built on and continues in our country today.

After coming home from the 2015 Western Front trip, I was hungry for more. As someone with learning disabilities, I had never wanted to learn much about anything because learning was difficult, but Australian military history really interested me. So much so that I got to the point where it's pretty much all I talked about.

I approached my friend and mentor Margaret with the idea of her tutoring me to help me get through a university degree in military history. I had decided I wanted to become a historian at the Australian War Memorial in Canberra. Margaret agreed and before I knew it, I was enrolled at university.

Surprisingly, I performed very well in my first year at university. Despite my disability, I had passion and I had Margaret's support and guidance to help me through.

In 2017 things became too much for me. To put it bluntly, I had taken on too many things. I was building a house with my brother and I was also looking for a new job. I noticed a change in my behaviour. I was snappy, narky and just plain tired. I realised something had to give.

I put my university degree and my dream of becoming a military historian on hold. I needed to get a roof over my head and some job security. It was a good decision, because my brother and I built our dream home and I obtained an excellent job within the Rural Fire Service.

However, my thirst for military history had not been quenched. Fast forward 12 months and I, accompanied by my parents, was back on the Western Front for the 100th anniversary of Anzac Day for the Dawn Service at Villers-Bretonneux. It was 2018 and it was something special to be there on that morning, 100 years after the Anzacs retook the town.

I am one of the very fortunate few who have attended both the 100th anniversary at Gallipoli in 2015 and at Villers-Bretonneux in 2018.

This is something that I will cherish dearly for the rest of my life.

While I was on Mat's Cowra Breakout Tour in 2018, he said to me, 'Would you like to come along to my Mat McLachlan Signature Tour I will be running in 2019?'

I asked him what the tour involved, and he explained to me that I would get to see sights that you don't normally get to see on the usual Western Front tour.

I couldn't say 'yes' to him fast enough! Mat was true to his word, and I did get to see new sights and visit places that I had not visited before. Walking up the Dead Man Road leading up to the town of Pozieres and walking in the footsteps of the Anzacs as they did in 1916 was very special to me and the experience stays in my heart.

After two years of no international travel thanks to a nasty virus, I was more than keen to get back in the sky and go west again. During the pandemic, I had discovered that I had a relative on my mother's side of the family who was killed in 1917 and no one from the family had visited his grave in 105 years. I was very keen to visit the grave of my great-great grandfather. As I write this, I have literally only just returned from this trip with my dad, and it was one very special pilgrimage. It was truly moving standing at Frank's grave 105 years after his death and knowing that I was the first in the family to do so. There were other highlights of this trip, of course, one of which is that I got to lay a wreath on behalf of the tour group and for my family members who had died on the Western Front.

During the tour I interviewed the chairman of The Last Post Association, and he gave me the opportunity of closing out the Last Post Ceremony. I felt so privileged to recite The Ode after The Last Post was played on the bugle. This truly was the greatest honour of my life.

With Dad at my Great-Great Grandfather's grave at Beaumetz Cross Roads Cemetery, Picardie, France, 2022.

12
When in Rome ...

'And what seems to be the problem, young man?' the Roman doctor asked me in his very Italian accent.

Thank fuck, I thought to myself, *a medical professional who speaks English.*

I put my hands on my chest in a rather dramatic way and said, 'It's my chest. I can't breathe.'

'*Si*, I understand, however, you are breathing otherwise you wouldn't be here,' the doctor replied in an almost cheeky manner.

Given my condition, I wasn't in the mood for humour. I replied, 'I mean, it's a struggle to breathe. My chest really hurts, I feel terrible.'

The doctor nodded his head and put his stethoscope on my chest to conduct his medical examination. After listening to my chest and a giving me a few pokes and prods, he had come to his conclusion about my condition. I waited to hear my fate: surely I was going to die in Rome, all alone and with no family or friends by my side.

'You have a chest infection. Take these. One tablet two times a day. It will clear it quickly.'

He was not wrong when he said it would clear up quickly. That medication was the best that I have ever been prescribed. It was so good that within an hour of taking a tablet, I was feeling semi-human again. By the next day, I was ready to see the sights like a typical tourist. When I eventually returned to Australia, I told my Australian doctor about the chest infection and showed her the box of medication I had been prescribed.

'Ha!' My doctor laughed as she looked at the box that had once contained the magic pills. 'They are illegal here in Australia.'

When in Rome, do as the Romans do.

What do Romans do? Well, they seem to eat a lot, drink a lot and smoke a lot. I was on my big adventure, a whole six months overseas with only me.

Following my suicide attempt, I was learning to take stock of my life and step outside of what was normal and routine because obviously that hadn't really been working for me. Seeing that many of my friends had travelled internationally, I decided I would do the same. And I was shitting myself!

The whole idea of being in a country with a completely different culture, a different language, different rules and laws and different food was very daunting for this 22-year-old Aussie guy. My dad was not with me. No one was with me. A million 'what ifs' would run through my head daily during the lead up to my departure. What if I lose my passport? What if I get lost? What if I get sick? Well, as you now know I did get sick, and I got some shit-hot meds.

Talking about drugs, I was extremely hyped for my visit to Amsterdam. I had been told by everyone,

'Mate, the girls there are the hottest in the world and they all look like that.'

I don't know if it was just me, but I thought most Dutch women were average, at best. Now, I know I may not be an oil painting myself, but I can still have an opinion. I also have an opinion on the infamous red light district. It was a real letdown. Most of the girls in the windows were just there, looking down, playing on their mobile phones rather than paying the punters any attention. In hindsight, I really should have paid more attention to the architecture rather than trying to spot the hottest girl in the world. Luckily for me, when I ended up in Prague, I actually looked at the beautiful buildings instead.

While in this 'anything seems to go' country, I was on a Contiki tour, so I had some people to hang with. A few of us lads and two of the girls decided to give hash cookies a go. Now, at this point, I will remind you, that in Amsterdam, the smoking or consumption of marijuana is legal and a common practice, so tasting a hash cookie and smoking a joint means we were not breaking any laws. Yes, I ate the hash cookie. Probably not the most delicious cookie in the world, but hey, it was a cultural experience. And yes, I smoked a joint. We all did. The poor girls at our table, though, they ordered a whole joint each for themselves and after two puffs they were coughing their lungs up. 'You guys can have it,' they both said, handing their joints across the table to us lads who were sitting there just laughing.

As if eating a hash cookie and smoking a joint in public legally wasn't enough of a cultural experience for an innocent Aussie boy from Hazelbrook, I had to attend a live sex show. Of course, I didn't have to attend it, but it was on our travel agenda.

As a group, we strolled into the so-called theatre as casually as semi-high young foreigners could, to watch the entertainment. The first couple in the show's line-up came out and positioned themselves on a circular platform that rotated. It was like I was watching a couple go for it on an oversized lazy Susan that you have on your table in the Chinese restaurant you attended for Grandma's and Pop's 50th wedding anniversary.

During a break in the 'entertainment' the host asked the crowd if it was anyone's birthday. The two girls from my tour group piped up, 'It's his,' in unison, pointing at me. Before I had a chance to tell anyone that it was not my birthday or not even close to my birthday, I was dragged up onto the stage, basically pushed into a chair and a large pair of bra-cladded breasts shoved in my face.

I was embarrassed to be up there, in front of the audience, and once again I thought how I had been bullied into it in an underhanded way. I guess I could have said, 'No, it's not my birthday. I'm not taking part in this,' but then I thought I would have looked like a sissy in front of my new so-called friends. The rest of the show I will leave to your imagination, but let's just say it was fruity …

When I chatted to Mum via Skype the following day she asked, 'How's Amsterdam?'

I replied, 'A cultural experience.'

13

The Six Thousand Dollar Party

So, in this book, I've told you many things that I hope may help you in some way or another, depending on your own personal circumstances. Right now, I'm going to teach you a lesson I hope you ignore. How to spend $6000 in one night.

While in Europe, I decided to join a new Contiki tour to the Greek Islands. The Greek Islands is known as Party Central and unlike some of the other European countries, it certainly lived up to its reputation.

It's like there's just no laws in Greece! No regard for health and safety, which consequently makes for a very fun time. Responsible service of alcohol? What the fuck is that? Because I thought I was Richard Branson and handed my credit card over the bar, I was allowed to do whatever I wanted …

For the first time in my life, I felt like I belonged, and everyone wasn't just being nice to me because I was shouting the drinks. From the start of the tour, I had clicked with a group and they just accepted me for who I was. I wasn't shunned, I wasn't made fun of, and I wasn't bullied.

I felt at ease with these people. I remember being in the water skinny dipping with them (a definite first for me) and I wasn't worried about what they thought of my body. While we were frolicking free in our natural state, one of the guys from the tour group thought he would be funny and steal our clothes. Luckily for us, a Kiwi lass who was also skinny dipping saw the would-be thief and raced out of the water in all her naked glory and tackled him to the ground. The best part of this scene was the fact that she was not a large girl, but she lined him up and absolutely smashed him! We pissed ourselves laughing at what had unfolded in front of our eyes.

Coyote Ugly, eat your heart out! You should have seen me dancing on the bar. While on the bar with my mates I was holding a three-litre bottle of vodka, drinking from it, and then spraying it out onto the audience in front of me. Once the vodka was all gone, I ordered a few huge bottles of champagne magnums and handed them over to the boys on the bar who were dancing too, and we proceeded to spray them as well as soaking the partygoers, who were having the time of their lives.

I have never drunk so much alcohol in my life. I have also never paid for so many people to drink so much alcohol at once. Because I was Richard Branson, my group had table service and everyone just ordered whatever they liked. I absolutely thought nothing of it at the time; all I knew was that they were all having a good time and I was having a ball, something that was very unfamiliar to me, but I knew I loved the feeling. I felt free and I felt like me. I felt like the true Adam was finally breaking free of his cocoon. He was spreading his wings, trying new exciting things and actually living life.

'Last night was awesome!' one of the lads from my group exclaimed in our hotel room the following day after many hours of sleep.

'Yep, I reckon I've never had so much fun in my life!' I replied surprised by my lack of hangover considering the excessive amount of alcohol I had consumed. I then thought that was one perk of being a large guy, my body just soaked the alcohol up.

'How much do ya reckon that cost ya?' my mate asked in an inquisitive manner.

I jumped onto my internet banking and checked my account. Looking at the screen with the numbers in front of me, I said, 'Nah, that can't be right.'

My mate quickly asked, 'What is it? What's not right?'

I pointed at the screen and to the credit card statement which totalled 6000 dollars AUD.

'Holy fuck,' he said, almost laughing.

'That can't be right. That should be like $600 dollars, not $6000!' I exclaimed in an exasperated manner.

'Nah, mate. You spent that. You basically shouted everyone there.'

I rubbed my eyes and then my head. *What do I do now?* Well, I will tell you what I did. I cut my international trip short by six months. Yep, a whole six months of travel had been spent in one night. Unfortunately, I had no other option, I just didn't have enough money to get me through. As it turned out, I ended up not even having enough money to get home and so by the end of my time in Europe, I had to make one very hard phone call and ask my parents to send me money to pay for my flight back to Australia.

Back to reality in Australia, I paid back my parents with my first pay cheque. I'm not a moocher and I know my parents work hard for their money. Though I don't recommend anyone having a 6K party, I most certainly do not regret it. That party night was a breakthrough for me; the whole trip was. Though I didn't realise it at the time, it really was important to the whole self-growth process, the finding of the true Adam and the feeling of what it really meant to be alive.

14
The Body in the Boot

There's four people in my life without whom I would not have been able to undertake my journey – and be reborn twice. These people are my mother, my father, my late nan and my Aunty Merl.

Aunty Merl is now my late aunt as she has recently passed away. Merl had fought illness for the past ten years, battling until it was her time. She was as tough as nails with a heart of gold. She called a spade a spade and if you were a prick, she would call you one of them as well. You always knew where you stood with Aunty Merl and I liked that.

'I need your help, Adam. Need your connections to help us out on a little project,' Merl said to me over the phone.

My ears pricked up, wondering what the lady could be up to. 'Go on,' I urged. 'How can I be of assistance?'

'I want to get a mannequin and dress it up in military uniform as a tribute to our family members who served in the Boer War and World War I,' she said proudly.

Merl had always loved to chat with me about the family's

military history. She would speak of 'the boys' that served in the Boer War and in World War I and I would show her photos that I had taken from my trips to Gallipoli and the Western Front. She told me she would have loved to have been able to go on those trips with me if only her health had been better.

Having connections in the military and historical space has come in handy and I was able to make Merl's vision come to life. I did get a life-sized mannequin and a historically correct military uniform to adorn him, but the thing was, this body needed to get across the border and into South Australia where Merl lived.

With Mum, Dad, me and way too much luggage for a four-day trip, the mannequin had to be shoved into the car boot, in pieces. Driving into South Australia from New South Wales means you must go through one of the few state border checks in Australia. The border check is primarily for bio-security reasons and so when the officer approached the car he asked, 'Are you travelling with any fruit in the vehicle?'

'No,' I replied honestly, 'but I do have a body in the boot.'

The officer looked at me and said rather seriously, 'Well, I better take a look then.'

I popped the boot and the officer looked inside and started to laugh, seeing the disassembled mannequin. He walked back around to the driver's window and said, 'I'm glad it's just a mannequin. I didn't really feel like having to deal with that today. You are free to go.'

Once at Merl's we put the body together. Putting the body

together was the easy part. Dressing him was a whole other story.

'Looks like the lot of you are struggling,' my cousin Denise said as she entered the house for a visit. Her timing couldn't have been more impeccable because yes, we were struggling to dress the would-be soldier. But Denise worked in retail and basically dressed mannequins on a daily basis.

Within five minutes she had the mannequin dressed and ready for inspection. We all stood back and admired him; he now looked the part.

'Let's call him Sid,' Merl said.

We all nodded our heads in agreement as Sid was Merl's late dad's name. Sydney Clarke had served during the Battle of Beersheba in 1917.

'Sid's a quiet guest, he doesn't say much,' Merl would joke whenever someone asked about the mannequin that stood proudly in her home.

Merl always made people laugh, and me especially. She really got me and supported me, and she was quick to make sure that I didn't have my head in the clouds and that my feet were firmly placed on the ground.

'I'm proud of you and you will achieve whatever you put your mind to,' Merl said to me the last time I saw her before she passed. She could be firm and no-nonsense, but she was still very supportive, grounded and a loving person. Even though my Aunty Merl is no longer with us, she is always in my heart, and in the words of Helen Keller:

'The best and most beautiful things in the world cannot be seen or even touched – they must be felt with the heart.'

Oh, I almost forgot about Sid; don't worry about him. He is now standing proud at the local information centre, and everyone is still waiting for him to say something.

15

Unhappy, Unfit and Hating Life

I always wanted to be a better version of myself. It was five years after my suicide attempt and my life wasn't a bed of roses. Far from it. Though I hadn't killed myself, I hadn't vastly improved my life yet. I was still unhappy, unfit and very much hating life. Despite the fact that I had improved my relationship with my father, I'd had some amazing overseas experiences and I was learning to broaden my horizons, I still hated life. I hated that I hated my life and I hated that I hated myself, and deep down, I knew I could do better.

I was told by one of my few friends, 'Adam, you have to have the inner fighting spirt to want to change and to strive for a better future. It all comes down to you and you alone.' I agreed with him, to a *degree* …

Though I alone needed to physically make the changes, I needed support on my journey once I'd decided to make the change.

I also needed a good therapist. It took me four psychologists before I found the right one for me. I remember sitting there in front of him wondering what he thought of me. Would he judge me? Would he tell other people about me? If I told him things that I had never told another person, would he tell my parents?

I certainly didn't open up to him straightaway, but I was more comfortable with him than any of the others that had come before. He had dark hair and wore glasses that he would casually push up his nose after they had slowly slid down. He was only young, but he was very rational and straightforward with me.

After some time in therapy, I was finally able to be completely honest with him and 'spill the beans'. He didn't cringe or tell me I was crazy, what he did was really listen and offer valuable life tools to start my journey of self-healing and improving my life.

There was a variety of psychological strategies presented to me and it was made very clear that there was no overnight quick fix to break my negative outlook on life, and there was one very obvious elephant in the room. My weight.

I was the 160-kilogram elephant sitting there on his leather chair, hoping I didn't break it.

'Lose weight and your life will change,' the psychologist said to me.

I knew he was right. Being the size I was brought me down. People judged me. Hell, I even judged other overweight people myself! It is only human nature. I could deal with having red hair, I could deal with not being the sharpest tool in the shed and I could deal with having only one ball, but what I could not deal with was being the size I was, and neither could my health. And so, I was referred to a specialist weight loss doctor.

'If you maintain the lifestyle you have, you will be dead by 34,' the doctor said to me bluntly.

I just looked at him, wondering if he was pulling the piss or just trying to give me a hard time.

'I'm not kidding. I have your test results and they are not good.' He informed me that I had a blood sugar reading of 38 and the normal for my age was between 5 and 7.

'You are in stroke and heart attack country,' he said looking at me with stern eyes.

I immediately felt like a failure. Only five years earlier, I had decided not to take my life and to give myself a second chance and now I had blown it!

Instead of embracing a new chance to live life, I had just fucked myself over.

It's not like I meant to, but maybe I did. The same way I always give the enemy ammunition to use against me. Every now and then I would say to myself, 'You need to do something about your weight,' and then I would suddenly start the latest celebrity-endorsed fad diet or join the gym and attend two times but keep paying the membership for six months.

After having the big health truth bomb dropped on me by the weight loss doctor, I came to a realisation. I could just keep on going the way I was and live a miserable life for the next nine years or I could make a big change. I decided to take option two. That change was in the form of surgery. Gastric sleeve surgery. I was going to be reborn for a second time.

Fighting fires prior to having gastric sleeve surgery on 8 November, 2019.

16

Life-Changing Surgery

Forming a professional relationship with a psychologist that I could really talk to and who I would listen to had been a big initial step in my journey to make positive changes in my life. And I was about to find out that this was only a baby step compared to what I was about to encounter.

'This will not be easy,' my mother said to me as I told her that I had made the decision to undertake gastric sleeve surgery.

'Yeah, I know,' I replied, way too casually.

Mum stopped folding the washing and looked at me before speaking, 'No, you don't know. I am a nurse and I understand this process.

This will be one of the hardest things you will undertake in your life.'

'What do you mean?' I questioned, starting to listen to her.

'I have seen this operation go haywire. I've seen patients end up worse than when they went in before the op. The learning to eat again takes a long time. The whole process is painful. I don't want you to put yourself through this for nothing.'

'It won't be for nothing, Mum,' I said as I ironically downed a can of Coca-Cola.

Mum picked up the shirt from the laundry basket again and continued folding it neatly. 'It's your decision. You are an adult; I can only tell you of what I have seen.'

Four months from my initial consultation with the doctor I was admitted into hospital to have gastric sleeve surgery performed.

In the months leading up to the surgery, I had been placed on a strict diet of clean eating and exercise as I needed to lose 10 kilograms before the surgeon would operate. Now, exercise, that's an interesting word. My 'exercise' involved more than just getting from the sofa to the fridge. Naturally, I couldn't run. I was a large man and that level of exercise would almost certainly bring on heart failure. Instead, I started off with light walking. Even walking a few hundred metres outside was an effort. It made me hot and sweaty and short of breath. Dangerous stuff, that walking.

Being dangerous seemed to do me favours because I dropped a few kilograms. I increased the speed and distance I walked and kept up the clean eating. By the time I was due to go into hospital for the surgery, I had successfully lost the weight as ordered by the doctor.

When I woke up post-surgery on 12 December 2019 in that Nepean Private Hospital bed, I was in the most pain I had ever experienced.

'You might experience some side effects following the procedure,' the surgeon had said to me.

Some side effects, I thought. *WTF? This isn't just a bit of swelling and some grogginess, this is hell. I have died and this is my hell.*

I knew, however, that this wasn't hell because my mother was there. She was sitting by my bedside, holding my hand like a guardian angel that never left my side. However, my nurse was no angel. She was the devil spawned and had no place being a caregiver. This nurse just had the worst bedside manner. I was in all sorts of pain because gas was in my stomach and it was making me throw up, have the runs and the hiccups all at the same time.

I was beginning to think I had made the biggest mistake of my life.

I had paid $12,000 for the aftercare post-surgery and I was getting almost no care. After hearing the rude nurse once again talking about her patients, I let rip. 'Hey,' I said to her. The nurse turned around and looked at me with a frown. 'You shouldn't be talking about your patients like that. I can hear you from my bed. You need to work on your bedside manners or get a new job.'

I told the nurse what she deserved to hear, and then I got moved into a new ward. I only spent a few more days in hospital before it was time for me to go home despite still reeling from pain and having all those terrible gassy side effects. I was loaded up with drugs and kicked out of my hospital bed and sent back to my own bed, and this is where the situation became very real.

I was on a liquid diet for the first two weeks, now feeling the lowest I'd felt since my suicide attempt. The pain never seemed to go away, despite the medication, and sipping endlessly through a straw was depressing. I couldn't help but think of all the money that I had spent on doing this to myself – in total it was $27,000.

Now, you may be wondering, *Where the hell did a 26-year-old blue collar worker pluck that type of money from?* My super. Yep, my superannuation fund. Because I was in need of dire medical attention due to my weight, I was allowed to use some of my superannuation to pay for the operation and aftercare.

That was $27,000 down the toilet, I thought to myself. *Like my vomit, down the toilet. Like my shit, down the toilet.* When I moved off the liquid diet and onto pureed foods only, the vomiting and shitting became even worse. I couldn't eat anything without shitting myself. It was disgusting. I felt disgusted and I was still in pain. I was in such a bad way that I was almost re-admitted to hospital. The doctor believed I had food poisoning on top of the post-surgery complications and that's why nothing was staying down.

I was a baby again. Learning to eat again, as I couldn't do much for myself. I couldn't drive anywhere or lift any weight. I was so grateful that my angel of a mother was there to help get me through this very difficult period. Pre-surgery, my stomach was able to hold a litre but now, post-surgery, it was only able to hold 400 millilitres. A large part of my stomach had been cut out and the sleeve had been put in place. It took my body five months before it suddenly seemed to accept this package deal.

One morning, it was like God suddenly switched the light on inside my body and everything calmed the farm down. I couldn't believe it when I finally got to eat something and I didn't shit myself. 'Thank you, Baby Jesus!' I cried out loud to the Almighty.

Things got better and easier. I wasn't feeling like I had done 100 rounds with Mike Tyson, instead I was feeling like I could be Mike Tyson. OK, not really, but I was starting to notice the dramatic drop in weight loss and the distinct changes in my body and overall wellbeing.

I had lost 30 kilograms of weight in the first two months following surgery and another 20 kilograms by month five. Currently I have lost 62.5 kilograms of weight.

'You cheated by having the surgery,' I've had people say to me.

I didn't cheat, I saved my life.

I made a life-changing decision about my health that has allowed me to keep developing as Adam 2.0 – the newer version of myself. It was a major un-fucking.

The unexpected five months post-surgery truly were a major blessing. Even though I wouldn't wish that type of pain on my worst enemy, it taught me to 'harden the fuck up'. It almost certainly built up my resilience as well as my pain threshold. My living hell of continuous vomit, runny faeces and smelly wind showed me that I could endure the worst life could throw at me and still come out the other side. I was starting to develop my armour. My suit of armour had a shield of resilience and a sword of fortitude. I no longer was running around with a spatula of leftover cake mix and a spoon of sloppy ice cream. My days of cakes and ice creams were long gone, or so I thought …

17

You Are What You Eat … and I Was a Donut

'Addy,' my mum said to me in her motherly tone.

I spun around, a donut in my hand and asked, 'Yes, Mum?'

'You look like you are starting to put weight back on. You are getting round again.'

'Don't be silly,' I answered in a dismissive manner, taking a bite of the round, sugary deliciousness.

I walked off shaking my head. *There's no way I could be putting weight back on*, I thought to myself. I had paid a very large sum of money to have gastric sleeve surgery so the weight would fall off me. How could I be putting it back on? I mean, I hardly even had a stomach left …

Over the next few days, as much as I tried, I couldn't un-hear my mother's words ringing in the back of my head. I finally faced my fear and took a real good look at myself in the mirror and I weighed myself on the scales.

One thing about mothers is that they are (almost) always right. Mum was right and you know what else rings true? That old saying 'You are what you eat.' I looked at my body and I was a donut.

I had been trying to train but running was still not my friend. I have learnt that you cannot outrun a bad diet. Diet and exercise need to work in partnership with each other.

I watched a segment on nutrition by a well-known nutritionist named Samantha. I believed every word that came out of her mouth. She looked trim, toned and terrific and the woman was glowing, and by glowing I mean it was like her inner health was beaming out of her like rays of pure sunshine.

'Fuck this,' I said to myself, 'I haven't spent all this money to just put weight back on again.' And with that, I reached out to Samantha for help.

Reaching out to Samantha was a scary thing for me, not because she intimidated me or anything like that; it was scary because I had to admit to myself and those around me that I was struggling. Everything was meant to be good, and I was meant to be taking leaps and strides in regard to my health and wellness, not making poor food choices and headed back towards Depressionville.

To my surprise and joy, Samantha responded to my DM on social media. She asked me to send her an email to discuss my situation. I did as asked, and Samantha took me on as a new client. Now, originally, I was not intimidated by Samantha, but that was until I met her in person. Samantha had a no bullshit attitude and made me absolutely accountable for the situation I had found myself in.

'Not too bad,' Samantha stated as she looked at the results of my recent blood tests. 'Now, what have you been eating?'

I rattled off a long list of foods and drink commonly put into my mouth.

'It's all crap,' she stated matter-of-factly. 'Everything you have been eating is crap and is no good for you.'

I tried to rationalise and divert blame by saying, 'I've just been eating what I was told to eat.'

'Bullshit,' she replied. 'I'm going to change all that. I will have you eating clean and help you achieve your goal of dropping 15 kilograms to reach your goal weight.'

With her no-nonsense attitude, Samantha set me on a strict but surprisingly easy-to-follow program to lose those kilos. In the first eight weeks of being on the program I lost 7.5 kilograms. The hardest part at the beginning was getting into the right mindset. I wrote my goal down and stuck it on the wall so I couldn't ignore it. It was a constant reminder of what I wanted to achieve and why.

As the kilos started dropping off, *bam*, there was another pandemic lockdown! During what seemed like lockdown 5.0, I couldn't travel more than 5 kilometres from my house and Samantha couldn't see her clients, so I had to rely on what I had learnt to keep on the right track. Unfortunately, I don't do lockdowns particularly well and I have learnt that I really need someone in my face to help keep me accountable.

In the aftermath of the lockdown, Samantha assessed the damage. It was not good. I had gained 5 kilograms!

'Adam,' Samantha said to me, 'I will try to get you back on track but you need to keep doing the work.'

I nodded my head in agreement and to my credit, I have been doing the work. I have been training consistently and following Samantha's nutritional program. I am having a hard time budging those last few kilograms, but I know I just must keep at it and remember that,

'All progress takes place outside your comfort zone. You don't have to be extreme, just consistent.'

18

Getting a Good2Go Mindset

'You understand that this operation isn't a cure-all, don't you?' my doctor asked me, raising one eyebrow.

'What do you mean?' I responded, not really wanting to hear what I already knew would be his answer.

'I mean that you will still have a lot of work to do. You may not be able to eat how you did, but you will still need to make the correct food choices and you will have to have a fitness regime, including running, to help you progress to your weight loss goal and maintain that.'

Ah, I thought, *I fucking hate running …*

This mindset had to change, but change is never easy.

With the help of Samantha, my nutritionist, I had been able to change the way I viewed food, but I was yet to change my views on exercise. All my life I had associated exercise with pain and suffering. This is because when I did it, that's what I felt. I felt pain and I suffered and no, it never seemed worth it. It never seemed worth it because I never saw results and the reason I never saw results was because I only ever put in a half-arsed effort.

I hated running. I had spent a good part of my childhood weekends being dragged across the countryside to watch my brother Scott compete in his running events.

'Scott's such a good runner, why can't you run like that? Oh, that's right, you're too fat,' kids from my school would snigger.

The nasty kids were right, though. I was too fat. Well, I thought I was and so I had convinced myself there was no point in even trying.

It was now 12 months after my operation and I had dropped 25 kilograms. I knew that I needed to get a fitness regime happening and that I could no longer use the excuse that I was too fat.

I bought myself a new pair of Nike sneakers, so that I would look the part, and off I went to pound the pavements. I really didn't know what I was doing. I didn't know what pace I should be going or how far I should go. Despite now being lighter the pain and suffering of running kicked in pretty fast. I think I'd run only 800 metres when I became red in the face, sweaty and short of breath.

I stopped under a shady tree to try to regain my composure. I swear I could still see my house from my recovery position. I stood with my hands on my hips, my head hung really low, and I had a little spew. A passerby asked if I was OK, to which I just waved and said, 'I'm OK, just taking a breather,' as if I knew what I was doing. The thing was, though, I didn't know what I was doing and after a few weeks of almost dying every time I put on my running shoes, I decided I needed help.

The search for a personal trainer (PT) began. Unfortunately, it was now 2020 and Covid was on like Donkey Kong, which meant many PTs were not training clients, or at least not face to face.

I wanted to lose those 15 kilograms to hit my goal weight of 90 kilograms. I was failing on my own and starting to feel like I was going backwards. I had come so far and gone through so much that going backwards was not an option. I needed progress in my weight loss journey not just for my general health but also for my mental health.

I now truly believe that the right people will enter your life at the right time. First, Samantha entered followed by Sarah. Sarah was an army veteran who I had invited to come on as a guest on my podcast. Sarah was not just a veteran, she was also a fierce fitness guru and coach.

I needed a PT who would listen to what I wanted to achieve, but also understand my past, the journey I was on and my limitations. I didn't want to be constantly yelled at, but I also knew I needed someone who wasn't too soft on me and who would hold me accountable.

When Sarah agreed to take me on as a client, I was over the moon and my mindset started to change. Sarah introduced to me the concept of the 'Good2Go' mindset, which meant I was mentally in the right place to take on the challenges set out in front of me. So, each day I am guided by these words:

Willpower is like a muscle: the more frequently you train it the stronger it gets, which gives you a Good2Go mindset, ready to tackle any challenge or obstacle that stands in your way.

'I would like to see you take part in a triathlon. How do you feel about that?' she asked one day during a training session.

I laughed, thinking my coach must be joking.

Sarah looked at me sternly. 'I'm not joking. I know you can do it.'

Well, guess what? I am now training for a triathlon. My fitness regime now includes a swim, a bike ride and a run. I swim with a snorkel and yes, I do look hilarious with that thing on in the lap pool (I have worked hard at being reborn twice so I'm not going to let myself drown now!), but I know that I am swimming myself closer to my goals. I am always a hot mess after my run and some days I struggle to stay on my bike, but I haven't fallen off yet.

I post my fitness journey on my social media. It's not for the encouragement, although that's always more than welcome. The main reason I post my journey is for my own accountability. Sarah can see firsthand what I have achieved or not yet achieved. The whole world can see, but more importantly, I can see. I can't hide under a blanket of excuses.

I do also hope that my posting on social media (and writing this book), will encourage someone else in their own weight loss and fitness journey. They might look at me and think, *Hey, if he can lose 70 kilograms then I can lose some of my excess weight too.*

Working with Sarah has been wonderful for not just my outside appearance but also for my internal health. Her helping me shift my mindset has caused an almost radical change in my own mental health. When I started with Sarah, I was running 5 kilometres in 31 minutes and after only a couple of months training I have now knocked 6 minutes off that time and can run

5 kilometres in 25 minutes. I also have kicked some other big goals with Sarah including riding 25 kilometres on the bike and getting a new PB for the Beep Test at 5.1. When I started, I was only getting 1.3 on that test, so it's a massive improvement that I am very proud of. I can now swim 1.6 kilometres in the pool and it's all thanks to Sarah's training.

I never really understood how exercise made one feel good until I experienced what true exercise was and how wonderful and enjoyable it can be. The release of endorphins can't be substituted. Sure, I still have some mornings where I can hear the rain outside and I know it's fucking freezing and I just want to lie there in bed. The old Adam used to just lie in bed, and I remember where that got him – a one-way ticket to Depressionville. I wasn't on that train anymore. I was on a new journey, a journey where my destination was Adam 2.0: sunny, bright and not an easy target. And so now I throw the blankets off me and get my pasty white arse out of bed and into the swimming pool, ready to take on the world with my snorkel and Good2Go mindset.

With my fitness coach Sarah Watson in 2022

19
Finding My Tribe

'Are you sure you have not got yourself involved in a cult?' Mum asked me, raising one thin, arched eyebrow.

I shook my head and laughed. 'No, Mum, of course not. I've just been enlightened to a new way of thinking.

'Before you can achieve, you must believe.'

Mum looked sternly at me as she replied, 'Sounds like a cult to me. If you are looking to find Jesus, there's a nice little Anglican church down the road. Maybe you should go to that.'

It was in 2020 that I was first enlightened by Margaret. Margaret is not a cult leader; no, she is an inspirational and very wise woman. You hear keynote speakers and leadership mentors throw around this term, 'You've got to find your tribe,' but to be honest I didn't even know what that meant until I met Margaret.

'You will find your tribe,' Margaret told me.

'How? How will I do this?' I asked, exasperated. I did have Sarah and Samantha as professionals helping me with my nutrition and exercise regime, but nearly everyone else I would meet had only negative things to say about me or to me. The world just seemed to be overflowing with negativity. How was I supposed to find people who would 'get' me?

'First, you need to separate yourself from outside negativity. There are several ways that you can do this.' Margaret smiled knowingly.

I learnt from Margaret that I was allowing a lot of outside negativities into my life, and I could actually control a whole heap of them! The first thing I did was stop watching the nightly news. We all know that bad and dramatic stories are the ones the television media is interested in, and they also have their own agenda. Same with the newspapers, so I stopped reading the newspapers too. I also stopped listening to what I now know to be absolute garbage talk back radio.

You might think I went and lived under a rock, but trust me, if there's something important going on in the world, I still find out about it. What I don't hear about is all the shit that I just don't need to hear about.

My workplace at the time was a toxic environment for me. There was the bullying that I had become accustomed to, and so I hated going to work every day. Margaret spoke to me about how important it was for me to remove myself from such toxicity. She said it was poisoning me and she was correct. I built up the courage and self-esteem and finally left the job. Let me tell you, submitting my resignation was one of the most exhilarating and satisfying experiences. The look on my boss's and work colleagues' faces was priceless. They thought I would be there forever, forever their punching bag, but I had taken a stand and now I felt ten feet tall!

My love of motorbikes had seen me join a motorbike club in 2017. At first, I felt like I had found 'my people', people with the same interest as me. It didn't take me long to discover that those who were supposed to be my 'brothers' were stabbing me in the back (and no, it wasn't even one of those types of motorcycle clubs). With my confidence now at an all-time high, I decided to leave the motorbike club too – another carcinogenic environment – leaving their negative fumes that I didn't need to inhale anymore.

Suddenly, my life had been turned upside down. Jobless, hobbyless and mainstream-media–free, I felt most liberated I'd ever felt in my entire, short existence and it was showing.

'You what?' Pop asked, taken aback.

'I quit my job. The environment was toxic. I've applied for a position with the NSW Rural Fire Service.'

Pop, the old digger, shook his head, probably thinking how his unemployed grandson was going to be a moocher and a bludger.

Margaret said to me that when I limited my negative exposure, my life would change, and it would naturally start to invite positivity and the right type of people into my life. Enter Janine. Meeting Janine was a game changer for me. Even though I had taken some big steps in the right direction to improving my life, Janine was the reinforcement that I needed and a real force to be reckoned with!

Janine is a highly respected business entrepreneur and life coach. Through a chance meeting, I was able to speak with her and tell her my story. Janine listened. Yes, she really listened to me. I knew immediately that this was a person I wanted to work with, as I needed her positive, yet very real, influence in my life. I knew she could help me progress with my own development and help me grow into the version of myself that I knew I could be, the version that I kept referring to as Adam 2.0.

Janine is essentially my life coach in every sense of the word. She assists me in outlining my goals and we draw up plans on how they will be achieved. She kicks my butt when I'm being lazy, and I discuss all of my business decisions with her. When my eyes start to turn in and I lack focus, she refocuses me. She constantly reminds me why this journey is so important to me and how far I have come.

'What's the point?' I stated, frustrated at my situation once again. I had got it into my head that I wanted to serve with the Australian Defence Force (ADF). I was feeling fit and confident enough in myself to give it a go. I had wanted to join for a long time, but my weight was naturally always the main issue. Yes, I still had medical issues, but I thought, *Hey, I know others who have got in with medical problems so I will just try.* I also wanted to serve; though I was already working for the Rural Fire Service (RFS), I wanted more. So I applied to join the Royal Australian Air Force (RAAF).

'I'm sorry, but you have not reached the minimum level required to proceed to the next stage in defence' the email from Defence Force Recruiting read. *Kaboom!* Well, that's what it felt like in my head. I was suddenly filled with all these emotions that I hadn't felt in some time. The self-doubt came bounding out of the grave that I had buried it in, like a zombie on speed.

'The point is, Adam, you gave it a try and it's not what you are meant to be doing right now.

What you want and what you need are often two very different things.'

'That sucks arse,' I replied.

'Life is sucky, but not all the time. It's yin and yang, good and bad, and it's embracing this and moving on that makes all the difference.'

I knew she was right and I completely understood that the universe works in that way. How would one ever know what pleasure was if we had nothing to compare it to? But it didn't miraculously heal me from my feeling of failure.

'Am I wasting my time? Should I keep on writing this book or just park it? Should I give up on being a motivational speaker for young adults?'

Janine was silent for a moment, ruminating on my words. She then said, 'Adam, you have a choice, You either let this one event define you and go back to your old self and old way of thinking or you can move forward, understanding that this was a lesson and only one of many, many to come. The choice is yours. What do you want to do?'

'I want to move forward and keep my journey going. I want to keep developing Adam 2.0.'

Janine smiled and I smiled back.

Feeling trim and healthy with my mentor Janine Garner at the Manly Walk 'n Talk for Life Charity Day, 2023.

***

In fear of sounding like some spiritual social media influencer, I truly believe that the universe knows what you need and will provide it when required. Karolina is someone I didn't know I needed, but the universe knew.

I met Karolina virtually. I was looking to develop my sense of self, so I did what any young guy looking for answers does, I enrolled in an online self-development course.

While my mates were subscribing to OnlyFans, I was subscribing to myself.

Even though we weren't physically in the same space, Karolina and I instantly connected. Karolina had an aura about her that broke through the computer screen and the security firewall straight into my living room. I knew that Karolina had a superpower. Her superpower was essentially helping others to find theirs. I didn't know what my superpower or niche was, so I reached out to Karolina for help.

'You, Adam, have a very special and unique superpower,' she said in her Polish accent to me. 'Your superpower is your voice.'

'My voice?' I asked, not understanding exactly what she meant. 'I'm not a great singer or anything.'

Karolina laughed sweetly, shaking her head. 'No, not the sound of your voice exactly, but your message. You have a message to deliver and maybe even more importantly, you have a talent and a love for telling others' stories. You keep their legacy alive through the telling of their stories so they are never forgotten.'

Karolina's words were a revelation to me. I knew I had developed a passion for military history and now, with Karolina's guidance, I realised that this was my calling, my superpower, my niche, whatever you want to call it. Another skill I realised I had was that I was really good at telling stories and for the first time in my life I thought, *My God, I'm actually good at something* and that felt great.

***

'Mum really doesn't like that word, Brooke, and doesn't want it used in my book,' I told my ghost writer, Brooke, down the phone line.

I could hear Brooke laughing. 'Alright then,' she said, we will change it to "prick"; you were a prick of a kid.'

Yes, I have a ghost writer. You didn't really think I wrote this word for word myself, do you? I have no problems admitting that, as I'm not some celebrity with a big head who takes all the credit and everyone is amazed by because they have such a busy lifestyle and yet they wrote a book about their life …

Brooke isn't just my ghost writer; she is my friend. She happily did illustrations for the cover art for this book well before I engaged her writing services. My journey resonates with her as she has undertaken her own battles, having been born with Ehlers Danlos Syndrome and recently overcoming alcoholism. Brooke is at a place in her life where I am headed. A place where she is confident in herself and her unique differences, proud of her disability and abilities; and she truly doesn't give a fuck.

Brooke's wackiness and mad sense of humour has taught me that it is OK to laugh at myself.

'They used to call me the Freckle-faced fart machine from Kmart.'

'Oh, that's gold,' she replied, laughing. 'That's definitely going to be a chapter name.'

She paused and said, 'You know I'm laughing because it's funny and it's OK to have a sense of humour and see the black comedy in things. For example, I've been told my running style is comparable to an injured gazelle. I think that's fucking hilarious because it's true. I do look like an injured gazelle, but you know what? That doesn't stop me from running.'

The more I believe in myself, the more beneficial opportunities are open to me and I am meeting more like-minded people. There are others in my tribe whom I haven't mentioned and my tribe is not full, it's still growing. I only willingly interact with those who give out positive vibes without being off with the fairies. These people are positive, but they are also down to earth and very real. They understand limitations, yet also push me so I don't fall back into my old lazy habits. They create a beat that I can move to; a shame that I can't dance … but I'm going to learn.

Today, I believe in surrounding myself with positive and inspirational people. Another of my valued mentors is Jo Jackson, my high-performance coach and treasured friend. Jo and I are pictured together at a motivational seminar conducted by Tony Robbins in 2023.

20

Finding My Niche: Hey, True Blue

If you can't beat 'em, join 'em. Or more in my case, if you are not invited onto someone's podcast, start your own.

I had listened to a particular history podcast for a long time and I loved that podcast. I knew the host and he knew of my passion for military history, so I thought I would get asked to be on his podcast to broadcast and share my enthusiasm with others. I waited and waited and waited. The call never came. Finally, I thought,

fuck it, if I can't get on his podcast,
I will start my own...

Starting my own podcast made sense. I had enthusiasm, drive and, of course, my love of history, in particular, Australian military history. I wanted to create something I could call my own and show those around me that I could achieve this goal, and more importantly, show myself I could do it.

The host of the other podcast that I never was a guest on was very open and obliging when I asked him how to go about starting my own podcast. He could've chosen not to tell me anything, considering I was essentially going to be a competitor in the flooded podcast arena, but he was great and told me what technical gear that I would need and gave me some contacts at the Australian War Memorial in Canberra.

Though I had all the enthusiasm in the world, I had poor technical skills and absolutely no idea how to interview people. The podcast was off to a rocky start. However, it did have a good name and it was a name that I came up with by myself.

'I want a name for the show that represents all Australians,' I told my friend Margaret, who had agreed to be my academic advisor for the podcast. '*How about True Blue History Podcast*?'

Margaret smiled. 'I like that name.'

As well as Margaret, I also engaged the services of my mate Kyle, who was tech savvy, to do my editing. I can truthfully say that I wouldn't have a podcast without Kyle. He makes the episode sound fantastic and takes the stress of editing away from me. It allows me to focus on what I need to do.

There's another Adam on the podcast team. He is my investigative consultant. He is responsible for putting together the veteran biographies. He helps me form the questions that I ask the veterans and the historians and he also helps me with the introduction for the podcast. Adam is also a mentor and gives me the confidence I need to successfully host. With over 25 years in investigating and interviewing, Adam's guidance has grown the show to where it is now. Without Adam, Kyle and Margaret helping in those first two years of the podcast, the podcast wouldn't still exist. The success of the show is a team effort and I thank them all for believing in me and helping me share this important part of our history. We need to remember what has been sacrificed for our freedom and we need to learn from our history so as to not repeat the mistakes made before.

Getting my first guest on the show was a bit of pot luck. I had met Simon Louagie, the director of Talbot House, which is a part of the Everyman's Club in Poperinge, Belgium. The house was a rest centre for troops on leave. I asked Simon if he would be a guest on my new podcast and to my delight, he agreed.

When I listen back to all of my early episodes now, I cringe. I know how under-prepared I was. I was so naïve and blasé that I once had a guest on who had written a book and I hadn't even read the book before interviewing him. He called me out on it and it was a big lesson for me that I needed. Now, many hours of research and reading go into the podcast before I interview a guest. I remember that it is a privilege for me to be interviewing them and listening to their story, not a privilege for them to be on my podcast.

In the sea of history podcasts, I didn't want mine to be lost. I wanted to stand out and adopt my own unique approach. I have achieved this by interviewing not just Defence veterans but also historians, with the view of telling our current and future generations of our past, sharing a combination of both older and younger veterans' stories.

I have to say a special thank-you to Donna Bourke. Donna was the very first veteran I ever reached out to and she agreed to come on the podcast to speak with me. Without her saying 'yes', I do really think I would have struggled to break into the veteran space, because I was this new dude who wasn't even a veteran himself or a historian, and I had zero runs on the board. I was essentially a nobody in the podcast space.

'Why did you agree to come on my podcast?' I asked Donna after the interview had finished.

Donna answered with conviction, 'Adam, I was Army Intelligence. I had you summed up in five seconds. Your passion and your care for telling our stories is why I came on the podcast.'

Providing a space for veterans to share their stories and experiences is what the platform was set up for, but little did I know that helping the veterans share their stories would actually help me to confront some of my own personal pain that I had been bottling up for so long.

On a call to my mentor, Janine, I broke into tears talking about the podcast.

Janine said to me between my sobs, 'As much as the podcast has helped the veterans, it has also helped you, it has been a cleansing thing for you, it has allowed you to heal.'

Making the decision to jump into the deep end and go for it with the podcast has been the greatest decision of my life. Though, in all honesty, if I had known exactly what the workload was that would be required before starting each podcast, I may never have even started it at all. But now it is my labour of love and I'm so passionate about interviewing veterans and sharing their stories.

'You're dreaming, Blum.' My old workmates laughed at me as I sat with them at the lunch table telling them of my aspirations of starting my own podcast. Now, all I can say is that I am having the last laugh. At the time of writing this,

I have recorded 65 episodes and I have had more than 50,000 downloads.

Those guys, they are still where they were three years ago, in the same job and doing the same old thing.

The doors that have opened for me because I took a chance and backed myself to do something that was way outside my comfort zone and so foreign to me has truly been amazing. When we shift focus and go into the un-comfort zone, we undergo change. I did some studies on podcasts (yes, you read that right, I did do some study) and the average life of a podcast is seven episodes. What happens is that the person who started the podcast realises that there is a lot of work involved and the podcast doesn't make itself. Guests don't magically appear or knock on your door wanting to be on your podcast. Interviewing is not as easy as it looks and you need to do extensive research so you don't look like a dick. If a podcast makes it past seven episodes, it shows that the creator is committed.

The podcast has been a hell of a lot of work, but is so rewarding too. I sit back and reflect on some of the guests who I have had on and I feel honoured and blessed to have been able to interview these people. I have had a conversation with a World War II veteran. I spoke with SASR veterans and I have spoken to a serving senator. I have spoken with one of the first female commanders in the Navy and I have spoken with one of the original 2nd Commando veterans, the late great Warrant Officer Nick Hill, who became a close friend and brother – someone I miss dearly. I'm forever grateful that I had the opportunity to record his life and now his memory will live on forever through the podcast. I have chatted with the first female commando in the 2nd Commando Regiment and I have been lucky to hear the stories of combat medics and even a gold medallist Paralympian!

I have also spoken with combat controllers who were the very first in raising their Special Forces squadron and I have also spoken with the very first FA18 top gun pilot. I have spoken with war widows and I have been lucky enough to speak with Vietnam veterans. I have had the privilege to speak with the father of a Victoria Cross recipient awarded posthumously. I have also had the honour of meeting our oldest living VC Victoria Cross recipient and meeting another of our Victoria Cross recipients and the list goes on. Meeting all these people, engaging in conversations and listening to their stories, it's all because of the podcast.

Who I didn't listen to were the naysayers who told me I couldn't do it! I followed my heart and my passion. No reward comes without turning up consistently and doing the work. Most weeks I put in 16 hours towards the podcast including promotional work, reading up for the next episode and emailing potential guests. The show is a real labour of love and something that brings me joy. It gives me great joy when a veteran says, 'thank you for allowing me this space'; it makes me warm and fuzzy inside.

I am honoured be a part of keeping the Anzac legend alive and to honour the over 103,000 men and women who have made the ultimate sacrifice for our country. It is something that I hold close to my heart, and I will continue to tell our True Blue History.

They shall grow not old as we that are left grow old
Age shall not weary them nor the years condemn
at the going down of the sun and in the morning
we will remember them.
Lest We Forget.

With Queensland Police Service Commissioner Katarina Carroll at QPS Headquarters in 2023. I interviewed the Commissioner for my *True Blue Conversations Podcast.*

Author's Note:

During the writing of this book the name of my podcast changed from *True Blue History* to *True Blue Conversations* as I wanted it to be more inclusive of guests who were not just veterans or historians but first responders and everyday Australians with a story to tell.

21
Keeping Your Stress Levels Low

Take the pressure down
Cause I can feel it, it's rising like a storm

I've quoted those famous lines from the John Farnham song 'Pressure Down' because they ring so true to my ears and undoubtedly resonate with many others.

Over the past few years, I've felt so much pressure and I know I'm not alone. At 31 years of age, I feel pressure to have all my shit together and though I have gone through a major un-fucking of my life, I am far from having it all together.

When I was in my twenties, I thought that by my early thirties I should be working in my dream job, be married and be starting a family. I suppose I thought this way because that seemed to be what people had done in the past. I now realise that there was no way that was going to happen in such a short time frame given everything that I had experienced. I am still learning exactly who I am and in what direction I want to head. I'm still sorting out so much of my own crap and still on this journey of developing into

Adam 2.0 that thinking that I should have settled down with a family is completely unrealistic and, to put it bluntly, selfish. I would love to have someone special to join me on my journey of forging fortitude, self-development and self-discovery, but I need to be patient.

Patience is a virtue. Indeed, it is, but being patient is easier said than done. There is so much pressure coming in at all angles that I often feel I am being bombarded and I can't find cover. To be honest, though, a lot of this pressure is a result of self-exposure. I don't have to look at other people's social media, but I do. I sit there scrolling through their pages showing their perfect lives with their perfect smiles and their perfect wives along with their adoring fans and followers. As I look at their perfectness, I think, *If I just had a few thousand followers on my Instagram, I would feel better and everything would be different.* What a pile of crap! That's just me looking for some type of self-validation and deep down, I know it would make no difference to any part of my being. However, because other people have thousands of followers, it makes me want them and I feel pressure to get them.

Even writing this book, I feel pressure. I feel pressure to get words on pages. I feel pressure to tell my story in a way that stays true to myself, but also won't embarrass my family. Sometimes I want to write things, but then I think, *What would my mother think about that?*

I feel that life is often running on fast forward and I want to press the pause button, but if I press the pause button, I might miss out. FOMO is what it's called these days: fear of missing out. If I stop, then surely, I will fall behind? If I stop wanting the best of everything right here and right now, then I may never have it. If I stop posting on social media then surely, I will lose followers, and if I stop the scrolling altogether, then I may stop comparing my life, my podcast and this book to others … Imagine that!

I do want to press the pause button and I know I'm in control of this, but for a 31-year-old who has been surrounded by social media for a good part of their life, it's a big step. What I need, and this is probably true for most of my generation, is balance. One should be able to engage in social media platforms without feeling pressured to keep up with all the Joneses. One does need to have a certain level of resilience so that all the Karen comments out there are like water off a duck's back. One does need to develop understanding of the fact that everyone has a different lifestyle and that not all may be as it appears …

Creating real memories is important, not selfies and short videos of funny goats. Getting back to the grass roots, to what is real, is important, and for me, that is family and my true friends. What is also important to me is concentrating on myself; being focused on myself, but not in a way that affects others in a negative way. I have come a long distance on this journey of changing my life and being reborn, but there is still far to go, and I sometimes need to remind myself that Adam needs to concentrate on Adam.

We are drawn to the white noise and shiny stuff on other people's socials like magpies. Developing the self-discipline to not be roped into all the glitz and 'look at me, look at me!' jazz that invades our space and homes is a life skill in itself and one that really needs to be spoken about and taught from a young age.

At times, I've felt almost crippled by outside pressure. It's not like I didn't have enough going on with my own health, but on top of that, it seemed like the world was yelling at me, saying,

'You should look like this and be doing this and have this and if you haven't you are a failure.' I spoke with Janine about this and she said, 'Adam, don't worry what others do. You are unique in your own right and when it is your time and everything is in place, you will step out of the shadows and step onto the stage and into your light and shine.'

'Pressure comes from within and so must be mastered from within.'
– Ed Jacoby

Now, I realise that all the pressure that I feel is not actually outside pressure, it's all within. I have been influenced by outsiders and created pressure within myself to be something like them. Do I really want to be like them? No, I just want to be me, because I have worked hard to be the new me and I kind of like the dude.

22

Gratitude, Self-love and Other Lessons

Over the past nine years since my suicide attempt, probably the most important lesson I have learnt is that everything you do in life comes down to a mindset. If you don't have the right mindset, then kicking goals and achieving success will almost be impossible.

You have to want it. By want it, I don't mean, *Oh, I would like to lose weight.* The mindset needs to be *I am going to lose weight and this is how and this is why.*

You also have to own it. Own your thoughts, own your words and own your actions. Make yourself accountable and stop being the victim. Yes, there were more than a few times in my life where I was victimised for no good reason, and the disgusting behaviour of a number of individuals is not to be pardoned; however, there was much in my life that I could change. I just needed to get off my arse and do it.

It was 2019 and I knew that a change had to come. One morning I woke up and said to myself, *This is it. I have drawn a line in the sand. From this day on I'm going to stop playing the victim and stop believing the bullshit that I have been told and the bullshit of a story that I have created in my head. I'm going to start living a positive life.*

Self-development is such a wank of a word, but what can I say? It fucking works. I started to focus on what I could do to improve myself and hence improve my life. I knew I needed to learn ways of getting out of such a negative, 'everything is awful' mindset. As I mentioned previously, I enrolled in a self-development course and it was worth every cent. It was an investment in myself. I also kept on working with my psychologist and I was starting to learn new ways to shift my mindset.

As well as removing negative influences that I could control, such as watching the news and reading newspapers and listening to bullshit radio shows, I began reading books. You might ask, 'Adam, you have learning disabilities and ADHD, how did you undertake this task?' The answer is that I simply set myself 30 minutes a day to sit and read. This is now a daily habit. They say it takes over two months to form a habit and I believe that to be true. I've formed a habit with my exercise regime following this same notion. I remain disciplined to undertake my training and on the days that I don't feel like training I still get up and get it done. And in regard to my reading, I do want to get better at it and I want to learn more, so I read every single day.

Gratitude is now something that I practise. Prior to my journey of self-development and influence from positive people and mentors, I didn't even know what being grateful was. The old me would not have thought to thank the universe or God for what I have and what he/she has provided. I guess I didn't even think about some type of higher power or bigger picture outside of myself.

Before I go to bed every night I now say, 'I'm grateful for everything in my life. I'm grateful for my health, my family, my eyes, my podcast, my arms and legs, my hearing and everything I have been given so I can live this life.' By repeating this every night before I go off to sleep, I have put my mind into a positive frame and when I'm sleeping these positive thoughts are circulating through my brain. When I wake up in the morning, I repeat this process. This is a process that takes time. I do not rush the process of doing my mindfulness and gratitude practice. I have learnt that it's something not to be rushed, because if you rush it, it is not as calming and relaxing. Undertaking this process helps to start the day on a positive note.

I had a gentleman on my podcast who in 2011 was blown up by an IED in Afghanistan while on deployment. He said,

'The first three steps that we take in the day are the hardest three

that we will take in that day and if we take those three steps, we can face anything that day has to throw at us and anything that life throws at us.'

Through my self-development courses, I have learnt that we have a subconscious mind and it's within this subconscious mind that we do things. Our mind might be willing to accomplish something, but our subconscious mind will stop us from doing that task. How many times have you had an idea or wanted to give something a go and then you share this with family or friends and they say, 'Oh, I don't know about that …' Suddenly, your subconscious mind thinks, *I guess they are right, it's probably not a good idea. Who am I to think I could do that?*

It's important to stay true to your conscious mind. I'm not saying don't listen to feedback, but I am saying not all feedback is 100 per cent gospel. You see, your idea is something that might not be for them or they may feel as if it's something they can't do or they are just not interested in. That doesn't mean it's not something you can't do.

***

'Adam, I love you,' I said to myself as I looked in the mirror.

'I love you too,' my reflection said back to me.

Sounds crazy and sounds stupid, telling yourself that you love yourself, but it is another important daily practice that I have learnt to do. They (the experts) say, 'You must love yourself before anyone can love you or you can truly love anyone else.' Once again it all sounds like a wank, but I speak from experience, and this is one very true statement. I have lots of love to give, but now, I make sure I give a big part of that to myself first.

My daily routine of practising gratitude and self-love helps me continue to push forward and not let myself slip back into a negative mindset, self-loathing and victim mentality all of which led me straight into the seething mouth of the black dog.

The black dog can be so easy to succumb to, but I don't want to go there again and I want to try to help others avoid going there and not growing the population of Depressionville, so I share my story and I share what I have learnt to this point.

I hope I can inspire others to make changes and help them get from where they are to a better place. I recently was talking to a friend of mine and I said, 'I have walked through hell and come out the other side. I may have endured pain and suffering, but I have learnt that through these struggles, it has made me the person I am today. I'm grateful for these challenges, they have made me a better person and have built my character, my resilience and my fortitude.

Through adversity, I have grown.

Let's talk about confidence: through the practice of gratitude and especially self-love comes real confidence. Confidence is not to be confused with arrogance. They are most certainly two separate personality traits. When I was at a low point and had a very negative mindset, I had zero self-confidence. I didn't believe I could do anything at all. When people put me down, I basically nodded my head in agreement with them. I wouldn't have dreamed of leaving my job or starting a podcast or writing a book.

As my mindset began to change, so did my confidence, I started to get some real self-confidence. It's a funny thing, though; people around me were so used to my lack of confidence that when I started to believe in myself, I was told I was becoming 'cocky'.

'No,' I replied, displaying my confidence, 'I am not becoming cocky. I am becoming confident. I now actually believe I am very capable of doing and achieving more.'

I now understand self-love and practise it daily. I also understand self-worth and now I believe in my own self-worth and value.

The saying goes 'clothes maketh the man'. Perhaps not quite, but clothes are helpful. I used to dress down all the time. I would get around in tracksuit pants and an un-ironed and possibly stained t-shirt and that's not just around the house. I dressed like shit because I felt like shit and because I dressed like shit, I looked like shit and therefore once again, I felt like shit. The meaning on a deeper level shows that you can shape your behaviour and performance when dressed well.

As my mindset changed and I grew my self-love, self-worth and confidence I realised I was worth buying new clothes for. I went shopping and bought myself a new wardrobe including button-up shirts and even a suit! With my new look came a new attitude. I looked good and so I felt good.

Even though I have such a wonderful, positive tribe around me sending me all their good vibes and positive influence and expertise, in the end, I know that I made the changes happen. No one else made the changes happen for me. I did it. You must really want to change and want it so bad that you're willing to invest in yourself and put in the hard work. Making changes to improve my life has not been easy and has not been cheap either. I've spent at least $80,000 on self-improvement through my weight loss surgery, medical professionals, mentors and coaches, self-development courses, books, nutrition program, and fitness program, but it has all been worth it.

'Adam, I don't have that type of money!' I hear you cry.

As you probably have worked out, I'm certainly not made of money either. I was able to use my superannuation for my surgery, which naturally means I have very little super now. I went without other wants to pay for my self-development, mentoring and coaching. There have been many weeks where I have just scraped by. Despite my often-empty pockets, my cup overfloweth. My cup is filled with gratitude and love and I understand that I will make it through each hour, each day and each week and that each of these moments will bring forth new opportunities and new challenges, sometimes at the same time.

I truly believe that working on your positive mindset to assist your mental health is the most important muscle and strength-building exercise that needs to be done.

Your mind will give up before your body will.

And this is why it is so important to have a strong mindset and to build your resilience shield and forge your fortitude. If we work on our mental health and our mindset every day, we continue to build our resilience to help tackle whatever comes our way in life. These are the lessons I have learnt about building a positive mindset and overcoming the challenges that I have faced in my life.

'Trust who and what you are, and the universe will support you in miraculous ways.'
Alan Cohen

23
The Willingness to Serve

For a long time, I have felt like I've had a severe case of Imposter Syndrome.

I felt like a fake.

I truly believed that despite being employed by the Rural Fire Service (RFS), I didn't quite belong in the veteran and first responder community.

I have such a great love of our military history, yet I wasn't a current serving member or a Defence veteran. My brain used to tell me, 'Adam, you're not one of them. You're not like them. They are special, they have seen and done amazing things, they have been deployed overseas, they have experienced combat. You haven't, you haven't done any of those things …'

Shut the fuck up… This is what I would tell my electrified piece of meat – that is, my brain – but it would still try to drag me down and convince me that my own service was not good enough.

When a veteran would decline to be a guest on my podcast, I used to take it personally. I used to think that it was because of me. *They don't want to come on my podcast because I haven't served in the ADF or done some cool policing job …* I would say to myself.

Looking back, I now shake my head at such irrational thinking. Thinking it was all about me. Who the fuck did I think I was to think that it was all about me? People have other shit going on in their lives. Not every veteran has the time to sit down and do a podcast and some just don't want to. They are simply private people and don't want the world to hear their story. I'd like to send a big shout-out to a 2nd Commando friend and brother, the late Nick Hill, because he said, 'Adam, don't worry if someone says "no" to being a guest on your show. It's not a reflection on you, it's a reflection on them.'

In 2022 there were devasting floods throughout rural NSW. As a member of the RFS I was deployed five times to various areas of the state to assist in these emergencies. I filled sandbags for days, I cleared fallen trees and I rescued livestock stranded in flood waters. I may not have been carrying a Steyr rifle or throwing flashbangs to make an entry, but I do know that my public service is very important.

A common thread throughout the veteran and first responder community is that we all have a willingness to serve others. I have now taken my ego out of it. My mother and grandmother both had a willingness to serve and they did just that through their nursing and charitable works. When you take the ego and bravado out of it, then the underlying factor of all who serve is the same.

We are all willing to give more than we take.

It is a great honour for me to serve my state and community as a member of the RFS. It is also an honour to be able to serve the veteran and first responder community by giving them a podcast platform in which to share their true stories.

The public service–minded community is a great community to which I belong, and I want to personally thank all of our veterans, first responders and the broader service community who give their all in order to serve the greater good. This willingness to serve others is not only for their country but for their mates alongside them, for the neighbour down the road, for the farmer out west and for any person in need.

'The depth and willingness with which we serve is a direct reflection of our gratitude.'
Gordon T. Watts

As a NSW RFS crew leader, I experienced 'a proud brother moment' when leading my brother Scott as we fought a fire at Falconbridge in 2021. It was Scott's first experience of firefighting.

24
Falling Forward

Remember how my mum thought I had joined a cult? Because my mindset was shifting she literally thought I was being brainwashed. To be honest, that's what my brain did need, one big washing.

It would have been lovely to have someone lay hands on me and say, 'Child, son of God, spawn of mother nature and earth, you are healed,' but that didn't happen. My healing came from within and I was in charge of how and at what rate I could start to heal the deep wounds of the past, and to then start to move forward in a positive and much brighter light.

My healing and new way of thinking had a real dampener put on it in 2020, when the COVID-19 pandemic hit our shores. It was not that long after my surgery and I was still learning to work with my body and take in all this new information about gratitude, self-love, resilience, fortitude, self-worth and the mysterious ways of the universe when *bam,* the universe decided to throw not just me, but everyone, a curve ball.

As you know, my hand-eye coordination skills suck, so me

catching or hitting a curve ball is unlikely to say the least. This meant I didn't do the pandemic well. Family means everything to me and not being able to just go see them rocked my world. I had coaches and mentors I worked with face to face and now that had been taken away from me. People's businesses were going down the toilet and people were becoming unemployed. Everything seemed so uncertain. I went back to watching the news and listening to the same old story. I now know I shouldn't have listened to the mainstream media spin like I did, but there was just no escaping it. It was like there was suddenly nothing else going on in the world but this new flu strain out of China.

Amid all the financial instability and employment uncertainty, I decided to leave the earthmoving job I was in and go work for a smaller company.

The smaller company made promises they didn't deliver on. Though my former workplace was run by the devil in hi-vis, the pay was a lot higher than this smaller company. Suddenly I was on Struggle Street financially.

Doubt crept back into my mind. I thought, *Fuck, what have I done? I have thrown away great money, to come and struggle working for a company that isn't paying great money.*

It's funny how it always seems to come back to money. Even though the new workplace environment was better, I was now getting down because of my financial woes. I was under pressure as I had a mortgage to pay and I was falling behind big time. After paying the bills I basically had nothing left. *Shit,* I thought, *how am I going to get myself out of this situation?* I then remembered something I had been taught by one of my mentors and I had a new thought, *I can't go back, I can only go forward.*

Though the world seemed to be falling down around me, I was still changing and there was a new awakening happening in my body, mind and soul. My new mentor and teacher, Bob Proctor, had said to me, 'When everything seems to be falling apart and you feel you are losing the grip on life as you know it you are shifting your mindset and changing your life.'

It is through struggling that I was growing as a person and building a stronger character and more resolve. Bob also taught that 'if you can't find an answer in the small problems how can you solve the big problems when you are a millionaire?'

It is through the hard times that we find out who we really are and what we are really capable of and what we can endure, learn from and more forward from. Most people say, 'Make sure you have something to fall back on,' Well, I have a learnt a different saying:

'I only want to fall forward. I want to see what is coming and face it head on.'

This for me is so true because you can't always see what is behind you, but you can see what is in front of you and therefore you should always face your problems head-on.

For all your actions there is a reaction, and you must react to those. This was one big lesson I learnt from starting a new job in the earthmoving industry during the pandemic.

That bitch, Rona, dragged her arse into 2021 and more lockdowns happened and then there was more financial uncertainty and the world seemed to be going right up shit creek. I was working on myself as much as I could, but I was not making ends meet, so I made another big decision. I needed a change. I needed to leave earthmoving altogether so that's when I applied for the Rural Fire Service (RFS) in the Mitigation Program.

With what seemed like the end of the world coming, I made it through the recruitment process! What my brother and I didn't see coming was the birth of my niece, Matilda. This caused both our worlds to be turned upside down. This sudden change meant we had to sell the dream house that we built together.

So, just as we put the house on the market, the Covid pandemic made a reappearance after a little down time and we were now in what seemed to be lockdown 10.0. This was all going on while I was training at the RFS academy for my new role. After only three weeks at the academy, my local government area was placed into lockdown, which meant I couldn't even attend the training.

This now started a new period of uncertainty for me. I couldn't just step back into the construction industry because that had been shut down due to the spread of the new Delta strain. I wasn't allowed to leave my LGA and to say I was worried is an understatement.

'Hallelulah!' I sung to the heavens when the government brought in the JobKeeper benefit. JobKeeper meant I would receive a weekly allowance from the government to help pay the bills while we were in lockdowns. I needed the money to keep paying the mortgage as we hadn't sold the house yet.

So, I had three months off. I was hoping the house would sell because despite the lockdowns, the real estate market was booming and the prices started to soar. The three months were a chance for me to really start investing in myself. I knew I was heading in the right direction, but there was still so much growth, teaching and understanding to undergo if I was to keep developing into Adam 2.0. I joined online self-development courses, I had Zoom meetings with coaches and mentors. As the weeks turned into months I was growing, changing and starting to feel more confident in the new me and the shift of my mindset and body.

Our house sold for a great price. But now I was homeless. I wasn't in a position to just go and buy a new house straight up so I moved in with some friends. Going from living in my large, gorgeous dream home to one room was extremely hard. Having to sell that house felt like I had lost an arm, like a part of me was gone. Obviously, I had a real attachment to it. I rang a friend of mine who's older than me and told her that I was struggling with my new living conditions.

'Adam, this is a wound and it's raw and you are grieving,' she said to me down the line.

'Yes,' I replied, nodding my head in agreement. 'You are right. I'm hurting and I don't know what to do next.'

She then gave me some excellent advice. 'Take some time and process what has happened and you will find your way again.'

Not long after that, the call came that I had been waiting for. 'Adam,' my new manager said to me, 'we are offering you a place in the Mitigation Program. You will be going back to the Academy next week to finish your induction and then you can start the following week in your new role.'

At last, I thought, *I have purpose again.* What this experience taught me was that without a purpose to get up, one can easily fall back into the doubt and negative thoughts of the black dog, the dog who waits in the background always eager to gobble you up. I had kept myself as busy as I could by working on myself during this pandemic period, but being a member of the RFS gave me real purpose and really helped all the parts of me that I was trying to work on.

'God's timing is perfect,' a Catholic friend of mine once told me. Now, I'm not what you would call a real practising Catholic, but I'm not closed off to this either. Something that I have learnt over the past few years is to be open to almost all things and most teachings. I may have learning difficulties, but I certainly know the difference between someone telling me something radical and extreme as opposed to something that I can deliberate on and that just may help me in some way. Maybe God's timing is perfect, because this welcome news about my RFS role came just when I felt really down and out about having to sell the house and I needed a new direction.

I found this new role was exactly what I needed. The people were friendly. Yes, you read that right, they were friendly to me. I was treated like a human being. Treated the same as everyone else there. The role was also challenging and demanding, especially on a physical level. I was tested on a daily basis. I had to use a chainsaw every day and given my lack of hand-eye coordination and binocular vision dysfunction, I was trying my best not to cut my hand off every day! Though it was almost certainly a challenge at the time, it did mean that I had to work hard at it and this is exactly what I needed to do. I needed to be challenged and I needed to show myself that I could do it.

There were plenty of times when I was my own worst enemy, like telling myself that when I got the saw jammed that I was *fucking stupid and couldn't get it right.* Talking to myself like this was me going into defensive mode, which is something that the old Adam did all the time. It's still something that I continually must work on, because in this role I am forever learning new things and I don't always get it right the first time all the time. But what I have discovered is that

it's OK not to get it right the first time. What I need to do is simply listen, watch, try and try again until I do get it right.

With my newfound confidence and a positive mindset, I recently applied for a crew leader role. Undertaking a leadership role and helping grow my new team is something that I never would've even thought possible a few years ago. And you know what? I fucking got the role.

If you'd have said to me five years ago that I would be writing a book about my life I would've laughed and said, 'You crazy?!'

If you'd have said that I would be in a leadership role with the RFS, have my own successful podcast and be training for a triathlon I would have said, 'Man, you really are crazy.'

Back then, I had no idea how much I would be able to shift my mindset from negative thoughts to a more positive yet real and rational way of looking at the world and at myself. I used to think that being unfit, unhealthy and unhappy was the way I was supposed to live my life. I thought this was what I had been served up in life and that there was nothing that I could do about it. It just goes to show how wrong a person can be about themselves.

I have now learnt, and proved to myself, that there is no challenge that I cannot handle. I mean, I'm here, telling my story.

If we don't challenge ourselves and get out of our comfort zone then we do not grow as a person. We stay in a neutral place and that's not where I want to be. I am now able to shift gears depending on what is in front of me. I now want to challenge myself every day and strive to be better than I was the day before, because that's essentially what life is all about,

facing challenges and then overcoming those challenges.

If life was easy and everyone was born the same the world be a very boring place indeed.

This coming May, I'm going to walk the Kokoda Trail to help raise funds for the charity Legacy. This challenge is so far out of my comfort zone and so foreign to me that I know I will have to draw on all my life experiences and on the mental health work that I've done over the past nine years to get me through this gruelling task. The same goes with my first triathlon that I'm about to do. I'm going to say it again:

the mind will give up long before the body.

I need to remember that as I set off on these challenges. Even though I may think I'm done, there is still more in the tank. It is these tough times that will inspire me to push my body and mind to new heights, and knowing that when I achieve these goals, I'll keep setting goals and keep striving to be better. I only hope to inspire others around me to do the same. Through all my learning and experiences, I finally understand that anything is possible and it's only your own thoughts that stop you from achieving. At the end of the day, it comes down to just how badly you really want it and what you're willing to sacrifice along the way. You need to ask yourself, at what cost do you want to succeed? For every reward there is a sacrifice along the way. I have made many sacrifices to be able to positively change my life and not be an easy target. I have lost friends, become like a baby again, endured physical pain and spent a lot of money. Now out on the other side, I'm a more solid human being for it and I know that this is only the beginning of great things to come.

'When you close the door of your mind to negative thoughts, the door of opportunity opens to you.'
Napoleon Hill

25
Getting Well

I was seriously going to jump off that cliff. I had the sole intention of doing so as I drove my white Hilux up that foggy mountain road, to my planned point of death. I didn't do it, but it has taken nine years since my suicide attempt to feel how I now feel. I know this is just the start and the journey of self-discipline, self-discovery and self-belief will never end. Just like Elton's John song goes, 'I'm still standing'. I'm not just standing, though. I'm literally writing a book about it all. I'm 60 kilos lighter. I've completed a triathlon. I'm a crew leader with the RFS and I have created and host a successful podcast. And the thing that is most important is that I feel well. I feel well in the head, well in the body and in the soul. Wellness in any shape or form is not achieved overnight.

Lots of people don't understand this. They think I'm all better and ask, 'How did you go from almost jumping off a cliff to doing triathlons?'

'With a lot of work, a lot of self-discipline, a lot of self-acceptance, self-love and a whole lot of good people around me,' I answer with a smile.

Control and power

One of the biggest issues I had was an imbalance of personal power.

To put it bluntly, I had none. I gave everyone in my life some power over me, especially those I shouldn't have. For example, that one kid from school who would undermine me at every opportunity and belittle me in front of his peers every chance that presented. He thought he was a king reigning over me because I allowed him to think that. I let him control how I was living my life. I still get mad thinking about the damage that one person has caused. I'm also mad at myself, though; mad for allowing him to have that much control and that much power. I'm mad for allowing him to keep me down and not standing up for myself. Mad for believing all the nasty things he said about me and to me. Mad that I didn't have any emotional armour. I had no shield, no sword, no nothing. It would be many years before I would find that shield and learn to raise it.

Giving someone power over you allows them to control you. The bullies saw that I was weak and took advantage of this. I was weak. I didn't know how to handle life and what it threw at me. I was an easy target.

What I remember most about those first 21 years of my life is pain and suffering. There are good memories, mostly time spent with family, a few friends, and I have mentioned a number of them already, but for the most part, I just remember everything being shit. I felt like a lesser person because I knew that others viewed me as a lesser person. I was overweight, in a blackhole and suffering from depression and anxiety. Not exactly God's blueprint for humanity or a pillar of society.

Because I didn't jump off that cliff, I decided, and I will repeat that – *I decided* – that I did not want to feel this way anymore. I wanted to control my life and the way I lived it.

Seeking professional help

I sought out the help that I obviously needed. I may have learning disabilities, but I wasn't so dumb I didn't realise that the problem wasn't just going to fix itself.

My GP gave me a referral to a psychologist whom I didn't gel with. I asked for another referral. My GP handed me the second referral and it was the same deal. I needed connection and synergy with a therapist. I needed to make my dream a reality and it was not there. I went back to see my doctor and asked for a referral to another psychologist.

'Why?' he asked with a raised eyebrow.

I explained that I felt that I wasn't making progress. And I wanted to get better.

'Well, I'm going to write you out a new script for your medication with increased dosages to help combat your depression,' the doctor replied. His response wasn't what I wanted to hear and not what I truly thought that I needed.

Taking control, I said, 'No, that's not the path I want to go down. I want to get to the bottom of what is happening in my mind.'

Finally, my new-found persistence won out and he gave me a referral to see yet another psychologist. It was third time lucky and I found the one that I needed. This quack was straight up and straight to the point and he was about to help me change my life.

During our first session I told him everything that had happened to me up until that point. I detailed my suicide attempt and how bullies had tormented me from my earliest memory.

'I want to feel better. I want the pain to stop. I want to feel normal and happy,' I said to him.

He looked at me and said, 'Adam, you do realise that it's normal to not feel happy all the time?'

I looked at him with a bemused look on my face, processing this information. I had been so caught up in my own unhappiness, it had never occurred to me that maybe other people weren't always happy …

He continued: 'I do understand that you have been through ongoing trauma over the years which is now presenting itself in various forms. We can work on this, but it's not going to be an easy fix.'

My whole inside needed a rebuild.

The outside was also a shitshow, but the outside reflects the inside. Now, the outside, that is how the law of attraction works. Most people want to change the outside first before building on strong inside foundations. However, the inside has to come first.

I will be honest and tell you that there were times where I did want to give up and I personally thought that the whole psychological process was just a waste of time. But something inside of me wanted to fight the good inner fight. That is the tiger within and the voice of Nan Stanton that always seems to speak to me at just the right time. Maybe the voice of my nanna is the voice of God, as they say God's timing is perfect, but I always refer to it as Nanna speaking to me. I only had 12 short years with Nanna, but what I learnt from her in those years was to fight, just like she did for so many years. I had forgotten about her words and fighting spirit for so long but now I was remembering them: 'When you choose to fight you become empowered, Adam.'

I wanted my power back. I wanted to live a life of happiness and abundance. I knew that I had to fight to gain that right and I owed it to Nanna and my family to put in the hard work. So, I just rolled up my sleeves. I attended weekly appointments with my psychologist and we slowly began to work through my problems. What we discovered was that everything said to me as a child played a massive part in my negative view of the world. The kids who laughed at me in class, well, they all played their part in my story and led me to becoming weak in mind, body and soul.

I sat there in an expensive leather chair, pouring out my soul to someone willing to help and guide me, when he dropped a big truth bomb on me.

'Your weight, Adam, is at the centre of most of your issues,' he said bluntly.

Addressing the elephant in the room

My weight played the largest part in my mental health struggles and was responsible for my fucked-up life. I shouldn't have been so surprised, as from the age of six I'd endured the laughter of others. I was bigger than the other children and even as a child my body image was negative. I hated the way I looked. I hated the way I felt and to be honest I hated being on this earth. When people say that time heals everything that is a lie. Time doesn't heal anything. The mental scars are embedded within you. The scars from my childhood torment will never truly leave me. I now have them for life. Trauma is trauma, however you want to break it down. It's always going to be there, but what you can do is learn to deal with it and get on with life and not let it hold you back from living it. I certainly had to learn to do this and 'stop living in the past, man …'

From this honest dialogue within myself, I started to really learn. I learnt that just because I had been a victim of bullying, did not mean that I always had to be the victim. I realised that not everyone needed to feel sorry for me because I felt bad. I was guilty for the longest time of playing the victim. I acted that way for so long until finally I was told, 'Come on, yes it's bad, but you have to get on with it.'

I do not play the victim card anymore; instead I use what has happened to me to help others.

At first when the psychologist addressed my weight, I kind of ignored it. Not wanting to push me straightaway, the doctor put strategies in place to support me when I was struggling mentally.

'Go to your happy place,' he would tell me.

I would zone out and focus on my breathing, slow my mind, close my eyes and just breathe in and out. I still practise this and I take as long as I need to to calm down and stop feeling anxious. At first when the doctor described this breathing technique, I thought he had gone mad. *You're meant to be a professional. I'm not doing that shit.* I was a 22-year-old male and there was no way I was going to embrace some new age Zen fantasy. We all know what being in our twenties is like. Everything that someone older said to you was met with, *Yeah, whatever. What do you know?*

But that voice sounded again telling me, *Adam, what do you have to lose? You have felt shit for so long that you have nothing to lose. Why not get curious about trying something new?* I listened to that voice and I did get curious and it turned out that my psychologist knew exactly what he was talking about.

I couldn't believe how much the breathing routines helped me with my mental struggle. It was like a weight had been lifted off my shoulders. I suddenly had a tool to use in the fight against the black dog. I couldn't believe that something as simple as breathing and slowing my mind when I was anxious could have such a dramatic effect on my life. I use this tool daily. I am so proud of myself for opening up my mind and trying something new, because it allowed a sense of positivity in for the first time that I could remember in a long time.

So, my weight. I needed to address the elephant in the room that was me. It was the linchpin, but I was still hesitant to confront this. Looking back, by not acting on his words about my weight, I added another year on to my road to recovery. With a clear mind you can achieve some amazing results, but when your mind is fogged over it processes things slower. At that point on my recovery journey, I still had a clouded mind and the process of thinking and rationalising was terminally slow.

If I'd had my mind open like I currently do, I wouldn't have had to wait so long to do something about my weight. But at that time I was self-sabotaging my recovery process. I wasn't truly listening to what my psychologist was saying and the very valid points he was making. He was giving me the advice that I needed to speed up my healing process, but whether it was stubborn pride or something else, I wasn't listening.

The doctor had had enough of my shit and I remember it well. He said to me, 'Adam, for fuck's sake, if you do not do something about your weight your recovery process will stall; until you address this issue your journey will come to a screeching halt.'

This made me sit up and listen.

I had not committed suicide and I had given myself a second chance and for the first time in a long time, I made a smart decision.

Disability is not inability

Another issue that impacted my mental health was the fact that I was 'different'. I had things going on inside my brain and with my body that most others didn't. As you know, with my ADHD and learning disabilities, I was behind the eight ball from the start. This was compounded when at 27 I was diagnosed with binocular vision dysfunction (BVD). This was a light bulb moment for me because everything that the specialist was saying about BVD made sense. It suddenly made sense why I saw things the way I did and why I had issues outside of the ADHD spectrum. The psychologist and I spoke about my ADHD and BVD. 'Yes,' he said to me, 'You do have disabilities that affect the way you learn and do things physically, but this doesn't mean you let them define you.

You are very much capable of achieving your goals.'

His words struck a chord with me. For the longest time I thought being a labourer was all I could achieve in my life. Now, I'm not taking anything away from labourers – I take nothing away from people who work hard. But I always wanted to do something other than labouring, but my disabilities held me back. I used to say to myself, 'Don't dream, Adam, you're too stupid.'

I had to work hard to change this mindset and change the narrative of my inner voice. It was frustrating at times, as I would try something and it wouldn't be easy or simple. Telling myself I could do something, then giving it a go was a hard process, and I was starting to learn resilience. I was learning to not give up just because shit was hard. The more I pushed, the better I got at it and the more I found I could do. I learned that my disabilities don't limit my ability to do and achieve.

Another part of the healing process that the psychologist and I spoke about was to accept what had happened to me in the past. Acceptance is important. He told me to, 'Learn from what has happened and use it to help the community.' Now, I have my own podcast and I'm writing this book. I can only hope that through my lived experiences and giving others a platform to tell theirs, I can help someone with their own personal struggle.

I built my confidence alongside the process of rediscovering my confidence. The black dog of depression doesn't like confidence. I found that out. The more I grew in confidence, the less the black dog came out from his den. People often mistake confidence for cockiness or arrogance, but true confidence is knowing your own worth by making clear and decisive decisions. It's the feeling of belief in one's own ability. Cockiness is being aggressive in your views and thinking that you are always right. That is not true confidence. Unfortunately, it was something that I was guilty of for a while, but as I grew as a person and opened my mind to new ways of thinking, I began to shift my frequency. The cockiness dissipated and real confidence took its place.

The fight

I have changed my mind, body and soul, and it is an ongoing process. Every day the black dog still stalks me, but now I know what to look for when its ugly head rears up. I allow myself to sit in the morass of having a shit day for only that day. I understand that when the sun comes up the next day I will get up and be positive again. I do not and will not allow myself to stay down for too long. I have to get back up; the journey and the fight is in me. I'm the one in control of my life and I'm the one who is the master of my own destiny. I'm not a victim, I'm the freaking captain of my ship, called *Adam 2.0*.

We are all the captains of our own lives.

We have the power to take control and steer our vessels in any direction we please. When the seas get rough, we find a way to navigate through them.

Nine years ago, I didn't lead my life, I let the bullies lead me. They were controlling how I orchestrated my life, but as I learnt, you can only do that for so long until something inside of you snaps. I snapped alright, but that day on the edge of the cliff was just what I needed to get me to realise that I needed to do something. Back then I didn't know how drastic that 'something' was going to be and I certainly didn't know how hard, both mentally and physically, that it would be. I've fought hard for myself, and for each new thing that I've learned, I am triumphant.

When asked if I am proud of how far I've come I say, 'Bloody oath I am.' And I'll never forget the people I have met along the way and the people who have helped me to become the person I am today.

My future is now so bright I need to wear shades.

26
The Outcome

'Change your mindset and you will change your life,' I was told by my coach, Sarah.

Ha, I thought to myself. *So, it's really just that easy, hey?* But as you've read, changing my mindset wasn't at all that easy. It meant I had to drag my arse out of bed when it seemed like everyone else was still sleeping, their heads nestled comfortably on their pillow while my big one was putting a bicycle helmet on it. I had to embrace the suck.

Though the changes seemed to suck arse, I started to notice positive differences. Subtle at first, then what I can only describe as life changing. I was changing my mindset and my life was changing. As this phenomenon unfolded, new people entered into my space. Truly good and amazing people. People who inspired me and continue to do so. Every. Single. Day. As you read in Chapter 18, my coach decided to throw a challenge out to me – I was going to tackle a triathlon. I remember when she told me that and I thought, *You're crazy. I can't do that and I don't want to do that, that's really hard …* I could have easily thrown myself on the ground and had a full-blown tantrum as if I were a three-year-old that had been denied a lolly while at the supermarket. I stopped myself, though, and took a moment to self-reflect, saying to myself, *Adam, that's the old you talking. You are not that person anymore. You can do this.*

My mind had started to heal and at the same time, so did my body. I started to train and by that, I mean really train. I was suddenly achieving things that I had never done before. I hadn't swum for five years. My large size meant that I hadn't wanted to be seen in the water. This had made me feel very low and sorry for myself in the past. After feeling like that for so long, it felt liberating to be in the swimming pool actually doing laps.

Now running, which had been one of my enemies, feels natural. I really started to train, but I was by no means an overnight athlete. I would run to a pole, then walk, then run again to the next pole. I increased to running to two poles. As my fitness developed, I extended the distances and kept pushing. After a short while, I was running a couple of kilometres, then three, then four. Now, I'm running seven kilometres in one run. It's been an amazing journey to this point: each new power pole literally is a goal post representing my own determination to keep moving forward.

I have had many setbacks and injuries, but these have also helped to build my resilience. When we face adversity, there are choices to make. We can either stop and wallow in the setbacks and injuries or we can choose to fight and push on when the times are tough. These times reveal who we really are. It would have been easy to give up and say, 'Well, my knee is stuffed, I can't train anymore,' but instead I went to a doctor who offered a solution to my knee pain. I had the inner fight in me; the tiger inside me had been awoken and it wanted to be stronger.

I was getting better at triathlon training because of my self-discipline. When it came to swimming, I used the same pattern as I did for running. I built up to my goal. One hundred metres in the pool then 200 metres followed by 500 metres then a kilometre. I was succeeding in my fitness goals and it felt great. It made me literally feel good and by that, I mean even though my body was often a sweaty mess, my headspace felt good. I felt pleased with myself and not just about the person I was becoming, but the person I was, there and then in that moment.

It took me a year to achieve my goal of participating in a triathlon. Training took commitment and I had to work hard in all types of weather conditions. It would have been lovely if the temperature was just moderate the whole time, but of course it wasn't. I would train in the freezing cold temperatures of deep winter. I built up resilience by jumping into water that was only 2 degrees Celsius, shrinking my manhood to near nothing, but at the same time, displaying the real man I had become. There were countless times over the past year where I would be running in the rain, telling myself 'skin's waterproof', in the words of former Commando and author Bram Connolly.

Lycra is not a word I would ever have dreamed of associating with myself, but here I was, pulling on my lycra to jump on my bike for longer than ten minutes and join the infamous (and sometimes hated) *lycra brigade*. However, I had no brigade with me, I didn't even have a troop. Hell, I didn't even have a partner. I had to jump on that bike myself, because Lord knows it wasn't going to ride itself. I had to do it. I reminded myself that I was responsible for my life and my own decisions. It wasn't anyone else's life and really, it wasn't anyone else's problem. These were my goals and it was up to me to achieve them.

I didn't take to the bike as well as I thought I would. As a kid, I seemed to live on my bicycle, but now, just staying on the thing was a challenge. Every bike session was a slow building block. I would build and then continue to build on the previous session. When I was partway up a hill, my legs burning, I would think to myself, *Why am I doing this? I'm not a triathlete. There is no way I can pull this off.* The black dog was stalking me with depressive thinking, always the opportunistic hunter. I do know that there were a lot of people thinking the same thing as the black dog and I can't blame them; my track record for starting things and seeing them through wasn't that great. I had always been a 'gunner'. Gunner do this, gunner do that. People were just waiting for me to quit again and the black dog was padding towards me, licking his lips.

What those people don't know is that with each physical training session, my mental toughness improved and I would yell at my black dog, 'Run back to your den, today is not your day!' And he would retreat, tail between his legs!

You need to practise what you preach; you preach about change, so keep changing. Keep challenging, no matter how hard it gets, I told myself as I suffered injury after injury. Even though I had lost a large amount of weight,

my body just seemed to want to fold, but I knew I needed to hold strong.

I had injuries in my shoulders and my ankles, and my left knee was giving me absolute curry. I was frustrated, but the lessons I learnt through dealing with those setbacks and overcoming adversity were invaluable. I even regularly started floating around in one of those new age float tanks. Very relaxing I must say. The muscle that really needed to be strengthened was my mental muscle. I needed to learn when to relax it, practise mindfulness and go to a place of Zen, and when to just harden the fuck up, princess. With my back to the wall, I kept pushing forward. Coach Sarah wouldn't let me play the 'I'm injured and everything hurts' card. She would change my training program to accommodate my injuries and I would just keep building on the training and working towards the dream.

The old Adam died the day I attempted suicide in 2014. Adam 2.0 was born, and had been slowly growing day by day, week by week, month by month and year by year.

I took stock of what was important. Though I wasn't a member of the lycra brigade, I did know I had the support of my family and Sarah. This support helped keep me going in the down times when I was frustrated with my injuries and other usual life shit. Sarah and I trained around my work schedule, which had become increasingly demanding. The rains worsened and I was deployed to assist with the flood recovery in western NSW. This made doing consistent training difficult and I had to change my schedule and routine. I had to overcome and adapt, to make my training regime compatible with work. *I can't take my bike with me on deployment,* I told myself, but now I realise that I could have, and I wish I'd taken it.

I was deployed for a month and I'm proud to say I didn't stop training. I found a way. I also trained through the Christmas period, which required some real discipline given the food, drink and merriness of family and friends. I wanted to just be on the couch, laughing with family, punch in hand, but I knew that wasn't going to help me from not drowning in the choppy, open water swim leg.

***

In January 2023 I took part in a promotion course for work and once again, my training routine was pulled out from under me. Sarah maintained my focus on the long-term goal – The Husky Triathlon Festival Men's Sprint Triathlon held in the picturesque Jervis Bay region.

In the lead-up to the Husky Tri, I wasn't feeling all that confident, as I was experiencing severe pain in my left knee and ankle. It was the worst that I'd felt up until that point. I kept cramping all the time and for months I had been battling patella tendonitis. I had been seeing a specialist for treatment, but then four weeks out from the Husky Tri, the pain returned.

As the day of the triathlon approached, I worried that my knee was going to give out. Waves of doubt flooded into my mind. That black dog stuck his head out of his den to remind me that I could fail, and everyone would say, 'Ah, there's the old Adam, he's back. That's the guy who says he is going to do something and fails, again.'

Fuck it and fuck you, I told myself, and right then and there I made the decision to go for it. I was going to give it my all even if my knee did blow out during the race. I was already a winner.

I reminded myself of the saying,

'The only failure is not to try.'

On the morning of the triathlon, to describe myself as nervous would be an understatement. I watched fit and focused people bent on smashing personal bests. They fiddled with their bikes and stretched their lean bodies like they knew what they were doing.

My coach Sarah arrived and bounced up to me with a big smile on her face. 'Adam!' she exclaimed, beaming. 'How are you feeling?'

'To be honest, I'm shitting myself and I'm wondering if this was such a great idea,' I looked at the ground, hoping it might gobble me up.

Sarah smiled warmly and said, 'Adam, you have done the training, you have done all the hard yards. Now, this is just another training session. Go out and enjoy. You will smash it. I believe in you.'

Those simple words sent the black dog on its way, whimpering.

As the start time of the race got closer my nerves really set in. I'd never set up the transition of going from swim to bike to run before. In hindsight, I should have thought it through. When I arrived at the transition point, I was amazed at the support I got from so many people. They made me feel a part of some wonderful triathlon family, all just happy to be there. I wandered up to the point where you need to rack your bike and start setting up my gear for the race. I didn't know what to do and it must have showed because the guys next to me helped me set up my gear and prepare myself. I was starting to feel better. I attended the race brief and now it was go time! Over a year in the making to get to this pivotal point in my life. My friend Brooke was there to support me. She gave me one last cheer of encouragement and it was game on.

As I looked around, I realised there were so many people who, like me, were doing their first triathlon. I wasn't alone, far from it. As I moved closer and closer to the water my nerves started to ease. I focused on the ocean and on the task at hand.

Splash. I dived into the water and I started to swim. The water was a moderate temperature. I immediately realised that this was going to be harder than I had first thought. I had only swum in a pool. The open water was choppy, real choppy, and I had to work harder than ever to keep pushing through the waves. Every time I went to take a breath a wave hit me, making it harder and harder to draw in vital air. I steeled myself with the thought that I could give up or I could keep going. So, I kept going. I took it one stroke at a time.

As I entered the home stretch, I started to cramp badly. I almost thought I wasn't going to make it. I was thinking my race was over before it had even begun. *Okay, Adam, you will have to take it easy in this last part of the swim and maybe the cramp will free up once you hit the bike leg of the race.* I made it through the swim and out of the water, then jogged towards the bike transition area, but unfortunately the cramp didn't free up. The tight crippling clench of the cramp just wouldn't let go and was getting worse. On the bike I was fighting the cramp and couldn't push in my full rhythm. I had to change my style to keep going. As I was riding, I stayed focused on the goal and visualised the finish line. Pushing through and not giving up consumed me. During this testing time I was using the resilience I had built in my training which I didn't know I had up to that point.

I dug deep. When I felt that I had nothing left I kept pushing and kept digging deeper and deeper into my mental reserves. The only thing that mattered right now was finishing this triathlon.

I no longer cared about times or personal bests. I had set the intention that I was going to finish the triathlon in one hour and

45 minutes, but I didn't care about that anymore. I just wanted to finish what I had started, however long it took me.

I focused on achieving a strong transition from the bike to the run. With every pedal I was getting closer and closer to the changeover. The last part of the bike leg was tough for me and I just kept telling myself to *keep pedalling, mate, keep going.* As I rose back into the crowded area, people's cheering encouraged me to keep pushing. I heard Brooke, and I heard Sarah say, 'Go, Adam, you got this! You're looking strong! Keep it up!'

As I transitioned into the run stage my leg continued to cramp. As I started to run, I knew it was going to take every bit of my new-found mental toughness to push through and finish the race. As I ran out along the 5-kilometre track I saw people stop, bend over with hands on hips and start slowly walking. I ran past them. Our minds give up long before our bodies do. If you have mental resilience to keep pushing on, you will be amazed at how far you can push your body.

As I ran I heard a young kid yell from the side of the running track. He called out to me, 'keep going, legend, you got this.' Support from a stranger is magic. I needed to hear those words of encouragement. As I turned for home in the heat, the sun beaming down on me making me almost drink my own sweat, I remember thinking, *all the sessions have been worth it.* I was about 2 kilometres out from the finish line when I saw a guy in front of me just stop. I could see the moment that he gave up. He threw his head back and stopped. I knew that I had the resilience to finish the race. I wasn't going to suffer the same fate. I knew I was in a mental fight and it was a fight that I was going to win. I had taken control of my life from bullies and slayed the black dog many times previously and I knew I was going to slay it again.

Let's call the last kilometre of the run 'Struggle Street'. It was fucking hot and I had nothing left in the tank. All I had at this point was a determined mindset. I had 400 metres to go but I felt there was nothing left. My tank was dry and the mental resilience I had proudly crafted was waning. Another competitor said to me, 'Come on, buddy, not long to go now. Four hundred and you're done. It's all flat from here.' Seems he had forgotten about the little hill. I looked up to the sky, reaching out to my nanna and said, *Come on, Nan, I need you now more than ever to help push me to the finish line. I need something from you, now. Some inspiration to finish this race.* She had given me the strength to pull back from my suicide attempt and I knew she would give me inspiration to finish my first triathlon.

At that moment Nan inserted into my mind all the bullies that had tried to destroy me in the past. That alone was the fuel I needed to finish the race. I let out an almighty '*Fuck you!*' to all the bullies and put my head down and arse back into gear. I closed in on the finish line. I could hear the crowd cheering. The cheering inspired me to keep going and to push on. I came into the home straight. I could see Brooke. She was cheering loudly: '*Go, Adam, you got this!*' I turned the final corner and kicked hard, finding yet another gear.

When I crossed the finish line, I looked straight up to the sky and with a big smile, I thanked Nan, the woman who inspired me to be all I can be, who taught me to have the tiger within and to fight to take back my power and pride. The absolute joy I felt when I crossed the finish line is something that will stay with me forever.

Sarah was at the finish line and she called out my name. I caught my breath and walked over to her. I gave her a hug and then cried in her arms. The emotion that I let out was truly uncontrollable. She said to me, 'I'm so proud of you. All the hard work has been worth it. You have worked hard for this result. You deserve this.'

After years of feeling negative and being told that I was worthless, I had come out on top. I was on such a high that the pain and suffering of the race was worth it. For the first time in a long time, I felt free. I knew I had achieved a massive goal. The last nine years had been hard, but I felt that I had climbed to the summit of a mountain. I achieved something for me. I had travelled the long road of pain to get to this point and it was my way of taking power back from bullies. I achieved something which nine years prior was out of my reach. I had proved to myself that anything was possible and I had practised what I had preached: 'The word impossible means "I'm possible"' and 'Before you can achieve you must believe.'

Right then and there I knew that I had turned a corner in my life. Finishing the Husky Triathlon had done more for me than I could ever have imagined. Although I didn't achieve the time I'd set for myself, I had finished the race in a very respectable one hour, 51 minutes. I spoke with Sarah about this and she was very proud that I had managed it under two hours. I know, though, that she would have been proud of me for just finishing.

We work on our bodies for various reasons, but often forget the most important muscle of all, our mind. This is probably the most important thing we need to work on first. If we have strength of mind, the body will follow. Getting out of my comfort zone was the best thing that has ever happened to me. I didn't realise it at the time, but when I agreed to do the triathlon I was taking control of my life again. The triumph of competing at Husky was the prize for all the hard work over the past 12 months. All the blood, sweat and tears were worth it and the tight glutes were just a bonus …

***

Discipline is the key. The ability to adapt and work around injuries is paramount, and having the mental resolve to keep pushing will make the difference. You must stay focused on the goal. What I learned was that my mental health changed through this process. I was feeling stronger mentally, I was eating the right foods to fuel my body, and I was allowing myself to rest. Those are the key fundamentals to achieving peak performance. They are key to achieving any form of success. I'm not saying you have to go out and complete a triathlon to feel successful, not at all. This is just what I have found worked for me. You establish what works for you. Be brave and step out of your comfort zone. Tackle a new challenge. Choose that one you have always wanted to do, and don't believe anyone who says you can't achieve your dreams. If you have a dream, protect it with everything you have.

Set your alarm, get out of bed and do the hard work needed to achieve the goals you set. I had the courage to be bold and step out of my comfort zone. I dared to dream that I could complete a triathlon and along the way I reinvented myself. The reinvention of my mind, body and soul was complete once I crossed that finish line. I know the hard work is not over and, in all honesty, it never will be. We are evolving creatures, always learning, always developing and always growing. I have completed the first of what will be many triathlons. I want to push myself further to keep building my mental toughness and resilience shield every day. With every new challenge I face, I know that I have the mental skills to face whatever comes my way.

I have learnt that I control the outcome.

I could have given up when I cramped up but I didn't. Because of my choices, I have this outcome.

'If you have the courage to begin, you have the courage to succeed.'
Harry Hoover

Taking control of my life, I competed at The Husky Triathlon Festival Men's Sprint Triathlon held in the Jervis Bay region in 2023.

27
Voices of My Tribe

Bec's story of growth

Bec is a marketing expert and she helps me with the branding of my podcast and to spread my podcast to a wider audience. Bec and I have since struck up a genuine friendship.

Bec has displayed true resilience throughout her own life, as well as courage and grace. Here's her story.

As humans we spend a lot of time comparing ourselves to others. I've had more people than I can recall turn to me and say, 'You're so lucky.' But what people don't know is that I have spent countless days and nights wishing I wasn't 'wired' the way I am.

I've always been both outgoing and loud, except for during a few shy years back in school where my insecurities about being 'the bigger girl' took away my confidence.

When you're an outgoing and loud person people assume it's because you are truly confident and happy. They never assume it's because you're busy hiding from how you really feel inside.

There are whole seasons of my life that I have tried to suppress and pretend they did not even happen. In 2020, my life totally fell apart and that is when I came to a realisation. I had no choice but to take a good hard look at my life up until that point and try to work out how I had got there.

Those who know me now would find it hard to believe that I have lived as a victim inside my own head. I had such a longstanding feeling of resentment inside of me directed towards my life, despite all I had. Inside I just felt genuinely hard done by. For this reason, life had to throw me a set of events to bitch-slap the silly out of me and give me a wake-up call.

This big wake-up call started me on my journey of resilience and staying positive despite the adversity that I had to overcome on the way. I still feel funny calling myself 'resilient', but my friends are quick to remind me that I am the one who made the tough choices when needed, and I am the one who followed opportunity with blind faith and courage to do so.

***

Brrrng brrng was the sound of my home phone ringing. My brother jumped off of the couch and raced to the landline telephone, picked up the received and said, 'Hello.'

I was only 13 at the time of this life-changing phone call. Prior to this phone call I'd been enjoying my teenage summer holidays, doing the things I liked such as playing my guitar, listening to my favourite musicians and reading books. My easy, breezy, dreaming-the-days-away life was about to change forever.

The news on the other end of that call was that my friend, Von, whom I called my 'sister', had been in a car accident and was in a critical condition in hospital. Overnight she had been airlifted to the Westmead Children's Hospital and was in an induced coma.

What followed over the next four months were hospital visits which are now all blurred in my mind. One thing that I do remember is sitting at a set of traffic lights just watching the traffic flow. I had this random thought that the traffic physically represented the poetry of motion that is life. Deep thoughts for a 13-year-old girl.

I couldn't understand the severity of the situation at this time. I didn't understand death and its permanence. I would spend my evenings in my bedroom bartering with God. 'God, you can take this if you give me Von back,' I would pray.

Von never woke up from her coma. I lost her.

My parents were like the British of old: 'Keep calm and carry on.' They taught me that death was a tragedy, but grief was bad. They held the line that we don't dwell on our emotions, that the feelings must be done and dusted once the funeral is complete.

Von's death was a catalyst for the beginning of my relationship with *avoidance*. Avoidance was the example my parents set for me at this time; this was the only way that they could deal with their grief, and they passed this role modelling onto me. For example, on the day of Von's funeral I clearly remember leaving with my parents and going straight to pick up my brother's car as if it was just another day.

This same rule was applied eight years after Von passed. My father was diagnosed with cancer and died seven weeks later. I avoided my feelings, made myself busy and didn't dwell on it.

This sounds like stoicism, but I know now that it was

avoidance. I would say to myself, *No one understands me, no one's been through what I have, I'm strong and I don't need anyone's help …*

At the time I didn't realise that all humans have their own stories of hardship, and it isn't a competition to see who has had it the hardest.

Because of my lack of ability to face my emotions head on, it was only 18 months after my dad's death that I started to have panic attacks. These attacks became a regular occurrence, and I would have up to seven each day. When you have a panic attack your body aims to release everything within it. I cannot count the number of times where I would be at a lunch or in an important meeting and then have to excuse myself to quickly find a bathroom for fear of literally shitting myself.

On social media I made my life look pretty awesome, but behind the filters and the big smiles, my life was a scramble of poorly managed emotions. I had angry outbursts and an inability to value myself enough to walk away from negative relationships or to even speak up when I should have.

My weight went up and down like a yo-yo. I had been diagnosed with Hashimoto's disease and I visited the emergency department on more than one occasion. I had multiple relationship breakups and heartbreaks to match. Despite being this loud, funny, outgoing woman who presented an image of 'happy and confident', I allowed myself to be treated incredibly poorly by boyfriends and friends alike. I truly believed that if someone was willing to stay in my life, I had to let it just be because I had already lost so much.

In 2019, I met Suzie. Suzie is a professional in her medical field and she kick-started something off deep inside of me which allowed me to make life-changing decisions. I had made the decision to seek out professional help because depression had raised its ugly head, and I was experiencing hectic suicidal thoughts most mornings as I drove to work.

When I met Suzie, I was 'happily' married. I was in a career where I was headhunted by other companies offering lucrative positions. I owned an SUV, ready for when I began a family and could be a soccer mum. My group of friends were social and *always* had something planned for me. On paper, my life represented a truly pretty picture.

In reality my self-esteem had reached an all-time low. This was a result of the actions of my husband at the time, but my mindset was that I was lucky to have him, because people always left me. I believed I was not a loveable person.

What I would learn is that my self-esteem, my victim mindset, and my negative thought patterns were the problem. Not my husband's actions.

I'm not saying my husband's behaviour was great – it wasn't – but it was my low self-worth that just kept allowing me to accept situations that were unacceptable. I believed at the time that was all I deserved.

'Our minds are like radios and we get to choose the stations we tune into.'

This statement by Suzie has stayed in the front and centre row of my head. It's these very words that kick-started me off into recognising and being able to reject negative thought patterns.

'Bec, I'm not happy,' my then husband said to me.

It was late January 2020 and ever since the ringing in of the

New Year, when we had drunk champagne together, I knew something was not quite right.

I looked at him and rather than resorting back to my old ways of telling him things would work out, I could change, and we could make it work, I said, 'I can't force you to love me.'

As soon as I said this, I had a sense of great relief shoot through me even though I was petrified of facing the reality of the situation; we both weren't happy. I had sat by and watched as he'd fallen out of love with me, but up until then I'd held on, thinking that having someone was better than being on my own.

All I heard about at this time was a new virus and the possibility of lockdowns in Victoria and all I heard at my work were gloomy putdowns. For the past four months I had been bullied by two of my managers and now these managers had called me into their office. I sat opposite them as my character was called into question. I was told that I was shit at my job and that no one liked me. I was then told to pack up my things and exit stage left.

Fired! I thought to myself. This was certainly new to me. In my ten years in marketing, I had never been fired. Hell, I had been headhunted for the role!

At this point, something very curious happened. I didn't go to the place of 'poor me' like I would have in the past. Instead, I found myself oddly excited by the prospect that my life had literally reached a new low. I knew I could now build the life I truly wanted, on my terms; one that I could build with intent. This fact coupled with the acceptance that my marriage was over meant that I now had new challenges in front of me. The difference being that I was facing these challenges rather than turning my back on them and avoiding the situations. Another huge difference was that I was attempting to face it with grace, and compassion for everyone involved.

Bravely facing these situations led me to leave the marital home, open a new business and start building a personal brand of my own. At times I thought making these hard choices would break me. There was a lot of crying. But understanding what lay ahead for me was a far greater prize than if I ran back to my old comfort zone.

Was I scared? I was TERRIFIED. I had built my entire personality based on my husband and being his wife. I had allowed myself to become basically 90 per cent dependent on him. Over the years I had been convinced that I didn't deserve better, nor could I get better than what I had in front of me. Now, for the first time in a decade, it was me, myself and I.

My life wasn't where I thought it would be, but I had made the important decision to learn from it. I learnt to understand and accept not just my own but others' shortcomings.

I will not lie; it is really painful and hard to accept that you played a part in your own situation.

It's so simple to project and place blame on others and say, 'but they cheated' or 'they didn't love me enough' or 'they lied to me in the job interview'. These facts may be true, but you can choose what you do with that information, just like I did.

When we choose to accept mediocrity, that's on us.

No path outside the comfort zone is easy and it's about learning how to manage our own mindsets. I've always had a sick fascination with pushing myself outside of my comfort zone. Because I'm a naturally fearful and anxious person, I really don't like the thought of pain or facing a scary situation, so it might seem odd that I often throw myself into things which I know will lead to many tears and/or breakdowns. When you achieve a mindset breakthrough you can prove to yourself that you are far stronger than you could ever have imagined.

My journey out of what seemed like a comfortable life has been full of painful experiences like daily heartaches, self-doubt, and bouts of deep depression. People talk about the glory that awaits you outside your comfort zone, but no one ever really talks about the pain you go through to get there.

Now, I am no stranger to putting myself through physical pain: I have run five half marathons, completed two triathlons, taken part in a three-day charity run plus competed in multiple fun runs, mud runs, etc. Anyone who has ever tackled endurance racing will know that a positive mindset is the key to success. Our bodies tell us to stop long before our bodies need to and that's OK, it's the brains way of keeping us alive. But it is our mindset that keep us in the race. I often think that life is like an endurance race that you didn't necessarily sign up for. Now here you are in a race without any training and you're expected to know how to navigate the course without any signs.

Over the past few years, I have discovered that the key is to face the hard stuff head on. When we avoid it or bury our heads in the sand and pretend like it's not happening, we close ourselves off to the lessons that lie within the pain, and the thing is, there is always a lesson to learn.

No one likes sitting in their pain. It hurts, it's uncomfortable, and finding out we aren't perfect can really bruise the ego. Real growth happens when you choose intentionally to live your life committed to learning and

grow through what you go through.

A positive mindset isn't something that we are born with, similar to confidence and resilience. We have a choice to 'flex the mind muscle'. It's a practice and a commitment to choosing to look at the world in a different way. In order to change you have to look at something differently, but firstly you need a level of self-acceptance. I had to realise that I was *choosing* my reactions to situations, which truly is often the hardest pill to swallow.

Hardship is inevitable. Hard conversations are inevitable. Sadness, hurt and happiness are all inevitable. Blocking out emotion removes us from truly living our life.

When you have that shit conversation in your business, in your career or with your partner. When life throws your plans completely out of whack and hits you when you are already down and out. When you truly feel like you cannot face that proverbial mountain in front of you, be sad and allow yourself to feel the whole spectrum of emotions. You can cry, scream and you can vent, but after that release, seek to learn, seek to understand and appreciate what is life. The 'rebuild' happens one step at a time, and remember that what we often think of as luck for someone has often taken years of rebuilding, one step at a time. Rebuilding, painfully but intentionally.

I can finally use the words *courageous, resilient* and *brave* to describe myself and I have rebuilt my life with intent.

Julie's story of hope

Julie and I met at an Australian Skin Cancer Foundation inaugural high tea luncheon. As a stage four melanoma survivor, Julie was the guest speaker of the day. Julie's story is one of never giving up and defying all the odds and succeeding when all hope seems lost. I hope you find Julie's story as inspiring as I do. Julie's story of hope can be read in her book Patient 71.

I had a beautiful life, not short of its ups and downs, challenges and fuck-ups, but beautiful all the same.

I had just turned 50 and was grappling with that number: '50'. The big five oh. It just felt, well, *old*. I was fit and healthy (or so I thought) and was training for an over 45's State of Origin touch football tournament that was about to be contested in the following month.

I was driving to work five days after my birthday celebrations and I distinctly remember practising gratitude. I thanked the universe for my family and friends, my home, my job and my puppy dog. You name it and I was grateful for it that day. Even my husband got a mention. I mean, I was having a particularly good day. Little did I know that within 24 hours I would be told I had months to live.

A couple of my colleagues and I went to lunch by Sydney Harbour. We were laughing and joking while taking in the sublime surroundings of the foreshore.

I meandered back to work that day oblivious to the life-shattering events that lay waiting minutes ahead.

Approaching my desk, a colleague asked me, 'What did you have for lunch, Julie?'

I stopped in my tracks; no words were forthcoming. I looked at him and managed to mutter, 'No words.'

He quickly ushered me to the foyer, obviously picking up on the fact something was very wrong. Then without warning, 3,2,1, my world went black.

'Julie, Julie, Julie,' I heard as I slowly opened my eyes. I could hear the paramedics calling my name relentlessly. I was just staring at the floor, and I felt so sick. I could hear them, but I could not speak. 'Julie, Julie, Julie.' They just kept repeating my name, waiting for a response.

I finally lifted my head and saw two paramedics on their knees trying to bring me around. My eyes made contact with theirs and I lifted my head a little more. I could see all of my workmates staring at me with their mouths gaping open. It turns out that I had just had a massive brain seizure right there in the office!

The paramedics strapped me onto a trolley and before I could ask, 'What the fuck?' I was in the back of an ambulance on my way to the emergency room.

After a myriad of tests and scans I was wheeled into a ward with three very old, sick people moaning and groaning through the night. I was in utter shock. How did my beautiful morning turn into this bloody nightmare? It would be 24 hours before I knew my fate.

It was around 5 pm the next day when a doctor flanked by two interns approached the foot of my bed. My husband, Scott, was sitting by my side.

Without hesitation he blurted out the gruesome diagnosis.

'Julie, you have tumours in your brain, both lungs, your liver, your pancreas and your lymph nodes and various other places. You have stage four advanced cancer, and this is not good.'

It took all my might not to say, 'No shit, Sherlock.' I knew I had just been given a death sentence.

I bounded out of bed, still in the hospital gown, and ran down the corridor. My husband quickly collected my things and chased after me. The doctor was calling out, saying, 'Hey, you need medication!' but I was running for the hills. I couldn't hear another word of this rubbish; it was too much, and my head was spinning. Apparently, I only had months to live.

We got in the car that night and headed to our beautiful home on Sydney's Northern Beaches and to my two teenage daughters, Morgan and Remy, and also to our beloved golden retriever, Roxy.

It was Friday night and as we drove through the suburbs, I was incensed by all the people hanging out in bars and spilling out onto the street. They were laughing and joking, welcoming in the weekend, while I was rehearsing how to tell my daughters whom I loved more than life itself that I was dying. Their mother was dying!

At home, it felt like everything had changed. The house felt cold, and it felt different. It even smelled different. I walk up the stairs to my room and lay on my bed and stared out the window into the darkness. I didn't know what else to do. Then I heard someone coming up the stairs. I knew who it was by her footsteps; it was Morgan. She took one look at me and her face changed to horror. I stood up and grabbed her in a bear hug and I said, 'I'm so sorry, Morgan, I have cancer,' leaving out the gory details.

'No, Mum, no, Mum, no, Mum,' she wailed.

My youngest daughter Remy came rushing in.

'I'm sorry,' I said as she just sobbed silently into my chest.

I couldn't handle their pain, anguish and their gut-wrenching cries.

'I'll fix it,' I suddenly said, 'I promise!'

I then felt a shift. I had always kept my promises to them and so they believed this time would be the same.

As soon as I made that promise I felt even sicker inside. *How the hell am I going to fix this*? I thought. *Oh God, what have I done?*

It was now too late to take back the promise, so I would just have to find a way.

After finding out my cancer was melanoma, I started my search to find any other survivors in the world but, sadly, there were none.

My head noise was ferocious … It spoke to me loudly: *You can't survive this. No one has survived this and you have promised your daughters that you would. How irresponsible of you*, and so it went on…

I started chemotherapy to buy me some time, and even then, there were no guarantees. I researched the hell out of the internet to try to find an answer.

I became fixated on a stage one clinical trial that was starting in the US. It was working with an immunotherapy drug called PD1 and was having some hopeful results in early trials. The drug was aimed at revving up the immune system and teaching your cytotoxic T cells to look for and destroy the cancer. I became obsessed. My gut was telling me I needed that drug; however, this would be easier said than done.

The clinical trial was being conducted at Providence Cancer Institute in Portland, Oregon.

After gathering the information and the contact details, I built up the nerve to call the hospital. To my surprise, I got on to the clinical trials nurse, Daniel. Daniel seemed rather fascinated that someone from Australia had called about the trial. At first, he sounded positive, explaining that they had had some reduction in tumours but did not have any long-term data to say how long this would last. He said he would talk to the trials team and I was excited at how positive he sounded.

Then came the rejections. 'No,' I was told, 'we're sorry, but you are not a US citizen.'

'No, you won't stay here for the full two years.'

'No, if you get sick here you are not insured.'

Then the clanger, 'No, we are at full capacity at 70 patients.'

But I would not let go. I was going to get into that trial no matter what because I had a promise to keep! I pulled out all stops and I would not take no for an answer. After three and a half long, stressful months as my life was ticking away, I eventually wore them down.

I became known to the scientists as 'Patient 71' and for the first time in my life, I was happy just to be a number.

That was ten years ago! I sit here writing this as a healthy 60-year-old who is fighting fit and cancer-free. There is always hope.

Change is absolutely possible: Keith's journey

Hosting my podcast True Blue Conversations *gives me opportunities to meet many amazing people from all walks of life. Keith Banks is one of those people. He is a veteran of the Queensland Police Service and a best-selling author of* Drugs

> Guns & Lies: My life as an undercover cop *and* Gun to the Head: My life as a tactical cop, the impact, the aftermath.
>
> *Keith's story is powerful. Keith has served at the sharp end of policing and I encourage you to read his books as there are lessons to be learnt that can be translated into everyday civilian life.*
>
> *Keith has become like a brother to me and is someone I truly value in my inner circle of friends.*

In August of 1987, I sat in my house in the Brisbane suburb of Enoggera. I was drunk, grieving and holding a loaded and cocked 9-millimetre pistol with the barrel in my mouth and my thumb on the trigger. All it would have taken was the slightest pressure on that trigger and my life would have been ended.

A month before, I'd loved life. I was a full-time member of Queensland's Tactical Response Group and had wanted to be in that group forever. On 29 July that year everything changed. Our team had raided a house to arrest Queensland's number one most wanted criminal, and he had opened fire on us, killing one of my friends and badly wounding another. Two of us had returned fire, killing the offender.

In the days and weeks since, I experienced what I now know was post-traumatic stress, anxiety and depression. I experienced flashbacks, sleeplessness, anger, sadness, emotional withdrawal and overwhelming grief. Of course, I blamed myself for the murder of my colleague and relived the events over and over in my mind.

There was zero counselling for critical incidents in this era and we were left to fend for ourselves. I drank every night and when I did sleep, nightmares would wake me.

On that night, as I sat with the gun in my mouth, all I thought was that if I squeezed the trigger, the pain would go away. My mind was suddenly filled with the recollection of a firearm suicide I'd attended years before and the brain matter on the wall left by the high-powered round exiting the person's head. I remember thinking how traumatic it would be for my partner to come home and find that. I removed the pistol from my mouth, unloaded it and put it down beside me.

I told no one about my dark thoughts. Who could I tell? Men didn't talk about emotions and I was not going to tell my partner, she was worried enough about me as it was.

It took 32 years for me to be diagnosed with post-traumatic stress disorder (PTSD). During that time I'd received three medals for bravery, resigned from policing to accept a senior corporate role, married, completed a Masters degree and been blessed with two beautiful daughters.

From the outside I had successfully transformed my life and had much to be thankful for. Few people knew the truth. I was battling depression (not that I knew it) and was constantly filled with anxiety and a sense of dread. I covered this with an extroverted façade; I was focused, funny, friendly and loved mixing with my colleagues and friends.

I drank too much and trained excessively to try to make up for it. My nightmares remained, although my flashbacks were reduced over time. My emotions were a roller coaster and I had to often hide my tears which would fall at the slightest sad event.

I was resigned to the fact that I had deep issues, yet I'd never associated them with PTSD before. I thought that was something experienced by the men and women who'd seen combat.

So, in 2006 I had a crippling anxiety attack, one that had no conscious catalyst and was totally unexpected. That night, at the urging of my close friend and mentor who was also battling his demons, I started on my counselling journey.

The next 13 years saw some improvement, but like many others I thought a few sessions would solve the problem. I'd feel better and then stop, fall backwards, find another counsellor, feel better, stop, rinse and repeat.

Finding the right counsellor is like searching for a partner. You go on a lot of dates and finally find the right person.

That's the journey of mental health as well. I found the right psychiatrist for me in June of 2019. After spending an hour with her for the first time, I flippantly asked, 'So, Doc, what do you think?'

She looked at me and responded with a sentence that changed my life. 'Keith, you have chronic PTSD and I'm amazed you haven't collapsed under the weight of it years ago.'

That diagnosis made me realise that my issues were real and not exaggerated. It empowered me to start my recovery and enabled me to start working on myself.

I started writing my police memoirs as part of my therapy and these writings have since been published in the form of two best-selling books. This success has enabled me to speak to a wider audience about the need to erase the stigmatism around mental health and continually reinforce just how important it is to look after each other.

I am honoured to be asked by Adam to contribute to his wonderful work and I understand completely just how his story is likewise part of his therapy.

Adam's journey is inspirational, and I know his message will literally change the lives of those who read it.

Change is absolutely possible, you just need to do the work, be authentic and forgive yourself.

Daddles: A short true story by Brooke Strahan

Brooke Strahan is a person who is like pure oxygen and is an inspiration in her own right. I have read the military autobiography she co-authored with Troy Knight, Havoc-06: A combat controller on operations *and just loved it. Brooke is also an illustrator, and has written a psychological thriller called* The Subject Trilogy.

Brooke has a special place in my heart because without her there would be no Easy Target.

'Prettiest baby in the hospital,' the midwife said proudly to my mother, placing me in her arms.

It was true, I was the prettiest baby. I was pretty because I had been a breach birth, which meant I came out backside first. Entering the world this way was not conventional, but then I never have been. Unlike all the other babies at the hospital, my head was perfectly formed and not all mushed up and dented; however, my bum was bruised.

I came out bum first because I was born with Ehlers-Danlos syndrome (EDS). EDS is a hereditary connective tissue disorder. I have what is known as hypermobility EDS or HEDS for short. It used to be known as Type 3 EDS.

Growing up I always knew I had an issue with my body, but

my condition was never really explained to me. I guess because even though my mother has it (not as severe) it was never spoken about to her and she just got on with it. Everyone thought it wouldn't really be any issue for me either.

The thing is, though, is that it was and is still an 'issue' (for want of a better word). EDS is a disability. It affects basically every part of my being. Some medical professionals class EDS as an 'invisible disability', but it's far from invisible in reality. One of the most noticeable symptoms was my speech impediment. My mother and her brothers had a speech impediment as did my brother. You see, we all have EDS in some form, I just copped it the worst and so my symptoms are most severe and obvious. After only a couple of years of speech therapy, my brother's speech impediment seemed to disappear. However, mine did not. It hung around well into my teens and it wasn't until I started vocal training (singing lessons) that I seemed to conquer it.

Growing up with a speech impediment is not fun. I was continually teased, especially during high school. I was also teased about the way I looked. I was tall and very thin. This lanky body type is common to people with EDS as many dancers, actors and models have a form of EDS. I was all arms and legs that went every which way as I am extremely hypermobile.

'Oh, you're very flexible,' people say to me. This is incorrect. I'm not flexible, I'm hypermobile and there is a distinct difference. I can bend all parts of my body in all different directions due to a distinct lack of collagen in the connective tissues. Essentially, I have very little 'sticky tape' holding me together.

My hypermobility is not just some party trick.

It is obvious in the way that I walk, run, sit and stand. It even affects the way I do things with my hands as the joints in my fingers are hypermobile. Sometimes, the most basic hand movement can be almost impossible for me. It's extremely frustrating not just for me but for others watching me, wondering why I can't do such a simple task.

My family gave me the nickname 'Daddles'. Daddles is a combination of the word 'duck' and 'waddle'. I was called that because when I walked, I waddled like a duck. This was due to the looseness of my hips. I am still Daddles and yes, I still waddle.

'Your running style resembles that of an injured gazelle,' a co-worker once commented after seeing me out on a run during a work lunch break. He was correct. That's exactly what I look like when I run. But I love to run and I'm not that bad at it despite my very unconventional form. When I was younger, I won most of my races, I competed in cross-country and even now, I still compete in triathlons. I know I look different and people still comment on my 'form', but I now have what is referred to as 'disability pride'.

When I was younger, I didn't have disability pride. I didn't even know that I was technically disabled. All I knew was that I had all this shit wrong with me. When I was asked questions, I didn't know what to say. I didn't know how to explain my condition back then and the fact that my family basically never talked about it didn't help the cause. They just used to laugh it off: 'Oh, that's just Brookie Daddles …'

No one at school knowing I had a disability made my life hard. The other kids knew that I was different and therefore because I was different, I was a target for their nastiness and bullying. I remember crying one night to my mum as I had been teased about my legs. Mum just looked at me and said sternly, 'Well, Brooke, at least you have legs. There are children without legs.'

You may think that was quite a hard line put forth by my mother, but she was correct. I needed to learn to be grateful for what I did have and what I could do. This attitude, though harsh for a child, started my journey towards building resilience.

As my speech impediment improved, my focus on my medical condition lessened. I guess I started to ignore it. Ignorance is bliss. I started martial arts training and became adept at the traditional Filipino martial art Arnis Kali.

I picked up this art form naturally and much to everyone's surprise,

I seemed to have a propensity for violence.

I had awoken some sleeping monster within me, but this monster had to be tamed. I quickly learnt that the martial arts are all about control and discipline. I needed to control my moves, my force and my rage.

One thing that was obvious was that I was strong. Here I was, an 18-year-old female weighing 58 kilograms and almost six foot tall, but able to take down my then 125-kilogram, six foot four boyfriend. My strength (that I still have) comes from the fact that my muscles and tendons work 24/7 overtime to make up for my lack of sticky tape to hold me together.

My abilities in this field led me straight into the security industry and then into the Defence Force. I naturally didn't declare my medical condition because I didn't think it was an issue. I mean I was strong, I was fit, and I could pass all the tests with ease.

Of course, it was an issue. After a major groin flare-up (flare-ups are common for those with my condition) rendering me unable to walk, I was put in hospital and suddenly being visited by all sorts of specialists. I was eventually medically discharged.

Now jobless, and feeling a total and utter sense of loss, I found myself back in the security industry. I also signed up with a modelling agency. I was a little like a not-so glamorous, not-so highly skilled Charlie's Angel. I had undergone a close personal protection (CPP) course and I was undertaking all sorts of security work including body guarding.

After a few years in the private security sector, I went back to working for the government, but once again, did not declare my medical condition. With all their background checks, they probably would have known about it, but if they did, I guess it wasn't an issue.

I worked for two different government agencies before going back into the private sector. I took a job in a very niche area of safety and risk management and I became a senior consultant for what is now one of Australia's largest companies.

I wore suits, heels and had a face done with makeup every day. I was a professional in a man's world. Nearly everyone I worked with was male.

My now husband and I moved to a little farm in the middle of bum-fuck nowhere in north-east Victoria. I was working remotely as well as having to drive many hours in to Melbourne to see my clients. After a few months, I could feel that something needed to give, and for the first time in my life I felt as though I could have some mental health issues.

I gave up my professional work and replaced it with a wine glass.

I started drinking all day, every day. I would rationalise my behaviour by telling myself, 'It's OK, you don't have to drive anywhere. You are high functioning. You still get your shit done and it helps your writing.'

I had started writing while still working professionally. I had never wanted to be a professional writer, an author or novelist. You always hear people say, 'Oh, it's always been my dream to write a book,' Well, that was certainly not me.

I did have some writing experience. While in the security industry, I did write a newspaper column for a year for my local newspaper. I had also contributed articles to industry magazines.

My fictional series, *The Subject Trilogy*, just appeared in my mind out of nowhere. The protagonist entered my head and she would not leave. It was as though a movie was continuously playing inside my brain. I could see the characters and I could hear their monologue. I finally gave in and started writing the first book in the series, *The Subject*.

Even before I had finished *The Subject*, the second book started playing in my head. My writing was improving, but my drinking was getting heavier. Before I knew it, I had a drinking problem. When I left the farm all I thought about was getting back to the farm so I could have a drink. My anxiety was also going through the roof. I worried about everything and it was utterly debilitating. I just wanted to be at the farm, wine in hand, checking on my animals and writing my books. I didn't particularly want to go anywhere or do anything else for that matter.

It is during this time that I really took stock of my Ehlers-Danlos syndrome. I connected online with others who had the same or another type of EDS and I learnt so much about my medical condition that no one had ever told me before. It was then that I realised my condition was something not to be ashamed of or played down.

It was a disability and that was OK.

My drinking wasn't OK, but no one had said anything to me and my husband was certainly my enabler. In saying that, he was also my reason to stop drinking. One day, after I told him that I wasn't feeling the greatest, he said, 'Maybe you need to stop drinking.'

I don't know what happened because previously, the sheer thought of not drinking seemed impossible, but I replied, 'OK, today will be my last day. Tonight, remove all the wine from the house.'

My husband did as I asked and so I began my sober journey. To be honest, it was a hell of a lot easier than I ever imagined. I had decided and I just stuck to my resolve. I will say, though, that I continuously walked around with a thermos of herbal tea stuck to my hand for a number of months …

My anxiety, which is my main mental health issue, has dramatically improved. I can now go to the grocery store without almost having a breakdown or needing a paper bag to breathe into.

I'm Adam's ghost writer, but Adam wanted to mention me in this book and he wanted me to write this section. That's the type of person Adam is; though ghost writers are meant to be in the shadows, he still wanted me credited and this is a testament to his kind heart.

It's been a pleasure working with Adam and it's been humbling to be able to help tell this courageous young man's story. One thing I have learnt through writing and telling others' narratives is that everyone has a story, it's just that some people's stories are more relatable and inspiring than others.

You can handle it with self-love: By a bona fide love child, Leila

Leila is a proofreader and line editor for my ghost writer, Brooke, and they make a formidable team!

Instead of writing about her own life experiences, Leila has focused more on her parents and what that generation went through and how the experiences of their own parents affected them. This was an eye-opening read for this Millennial!

The 1960s were a very different cultural era for my parents' generation. When they met in Geelong it was lust at first sight. My mother, Yvonne, was studying journalism on a scholarship when she met Dad, Wolfgang, the handsome German bike mechanic and popular drug dealer. Apparently, he had this fridge behind the bike shop's counter and it had everything in it – hash, weed, heroin, liquid LSD. Basically, you name it and it was available in that fridge. At the time none of this was criminal or considered illegal, and their generation really liked to party.

They were both children of parents who were deeply scarred by World War II. My nan, Myrtle, was a five-year-old in London at the time of the Blitz and lost many friends and neighbours, shelled by the Germans, in 57 consecutive night raids. On the other hand, Dad's mum, Hannelore, was born and raised near Bielefeld in Germany, brought up under the Nazis regime. Later, as young women they both migrated to Australia to start new lives in farming,

but the effects of the war never really left either of them mentally at peace.

It was natural for the children of this post world war era, the largest group of people born at one time, called the Baby Boomers, to do the very opposite of their parents. Some of the five million youth, like Mum and Dad, chose to let their hair grow long, seek love, peace and mung beans, and generally rebel against the social norms of the time. My parents did exactly that: they went together to the far north of Queensland and lived off the land near Archer Point, calling a tin shed near the beach home.

They were living free and just being themselves. Wolf would go fishing, shucking oysters straight off the rocks. Yvonne would bake bread and make homemade beer. It was a simple beach lifestyle and I was born in Cairns, a naïve and much-loved hippy child. It was a brief happy childhood full of nudity and the smell of marijuana, and it will come as no surprise to you that the advice I got when I left home at 15 years of age was 'don't smuggle drugs and don't take mushrooms because some people never come back'. Useful advice I'd say.

I personally don't use illegal drugs because I witnessed firsthand the long-term damage it does to emotionally vulnerable people, like my dad. Here was this fun-loving, capable, sensitive and artistic man who had violently abusive parents. As a result, he grew into a person who only wanted to be really liked. Hence the drug dealing. Let's face it, everybody really likes the dealer at a party. It was the 1970s, known as the 'Me' decade and was a time of explosive creativity, fads and crazes. The music at the time was reflective of the cultural changes and innovations that were to come in the 1980s. But by the end of this decadent decade many burnt-out and sold-out hippies were firmly on a path of self-destruction. Love was clearly not enough.

At the time, my poor mum did not understand that Wolf was suffering from deep depression. It was not even a word back then, and so nobody knew to speak about it. Their own mothers were silently suffering post-trauma and depressive behaviours. Neither grandmothers found a way to voice their uneasy mental health and they both coped with heavy addictions to alcohol and gambling. It wasn't until much later in life when my grandmothers would be prescribed antidepressants and anti-anxiety medication. There was no social dialogue yet on this hidden pandemic, no readily available resources to access guidance or therapists to help the traumatised. So, Dad got into self-medication and just went too hard at it.

Inevitably Mum had to leave Dad and his self-destructive behaviour for our own safety and wellbeing. We moved to Calcutta, India! Yvonne is an adventurer at heart and loves travelling. Looking back now I can reflect on two outcomes from the experience of those years: firstly, it made me resilient and tolerant of all people and secondly, I have been put off travelling all together and love staying home with a good book.

Growing up in Asia we experienced walking in the Himalayas together and travelling the Indian countryside by steam train. We would see villages that had never seen white, blonde-haired people before. Sometimes kids would grab my hair painfully, wanting a bit of it. At other towns we were revered for our differences. Once, I was proudly taken into a beautiful mosque, but because women are not allowed in the temple we were stoned out of that village in shame. Later, I would be run over by a scooter in the busy streets of Calcutta and I got concussion several times. One time, I watched the recently released movie *Superman* and thought that I too could fly, if I believed it enough, and so I leapt off a building roof… Ha-ha, this was probably my first lesson in disappointment! I broke my nose too.

When we returned to Australia my mother took her genuine love and compassion for people and became an advocate for cerebral palsy. She believes it is not what you can do for yourself in this world but what you can contribute to your community. I went on to study sociology and I received a first-class honour for my thesis on the rise of mental health in Western society, which was truly at pandemic proportions even then. Ironically, despite the silent anguish within my own family's life, I am the very opposite; I am possessed with a cheerful personality and I've always strived to connect positively with people. My superpower is my smile. It costs nothing and feels good to share.

Of course, life for Dad ended badly. After we returned from India my parents did try to reconcile. The love was still there for each other, but not the necessary changes needed to help his mental health and addictions. After a few years of phone calls and the odd visit, I did not hear from him for 18 years and concluded over this time that he must be deceased. Then one day out of the blue I got a phone call from him at work, and my angry response did not shock me in the least.

He called to say that he was in hospital dying of cancer and could I come see him. Of course, I did and it was a sad and tragic reunion. He was a full-blown drug addict. Even as he lay dying, his junkie flatmate came to score the morphine tablets he was stashing. In front of me, like I did not exist, they argued about where the spoon was. In disgust I rang Mum and said, 'Don't come see this, it'll just break your heart.' They spoke on the phone and he died full of regret at the age of 57, a very emotionally damaged and distracted little boy. Wolf never did learn to care for himself, because he was incapable of growing up emotionally and leaving his disappointing childhood behind.

I wanted to share my story as a cautionary tale. With the right support and communication, learning to self-love can help you overcome all of life's personal obstacles because you understand who you really are. When personal valorisation is achieved, you can think and act with the understanding that your own life is valuable. I wish to share an excerpt by the poet seer Hifaz from his piece *My Brilliant Image,* which moves me. I only wished I could've shared this insightful wisdom with my own family while they were all still alive.

I wish I could show you,
When you are lonely or in darkness,
The Astonishing Light
Of your own Being!

Tim Curtis' notes on resilience, fairness and sucking at life

I am forever looking for inspirational stories and self-help books to inspire me and I came across a book that has made a huge impact; The Resilience Shield: SAS resilience techniques to master your mindset and overcome adversity. *After reading this book I contacted the authors Ben Pronk, Dr Dan Pronk, and Tim Curtis to personally thank them. I highly recommend this book and again thank Ben, Dan and Tim for contributing to my own book and supporting me along the journey of building my own resilience shield.*

Dr Dan Pronk, Ben Pronk DSC and I wrote the bestselling book *The Resilience Shield*, which is an evidence-based methodology on how we can all build resilience. It recognises that resilience is a dynamic construct that can be developed. It spans innate mind, body, social and professional layers. It also recognises that *adaptation* is important in being resilient. Adaptation allows us to do things that we never thought we would be able to do.

Dan, Ben and I are all former Special Air Service (SAS) Regiment officers armed with MBAs. If you read our biographical summaries we would collectively seem somewhat noteworthy. Dr Dan was a professional triathlete before studying medicine. He's also an accomplished entrepreneur. Ben has graduated at the top of too many courses to mention, has been decorated for leadership in action and just ran a sub three-hour marathon. I have had some success in swimming and more recently made the All Australian Masters AFL team. My podcast with Ben, The *Unforgiving60*, has had some success in the ratings and our consulting company is also well regarded.

But,

we have all struggled to overcome adversity through our lives.

Dan and Ben with the loss of their father several years ago. Dr Dan with his personal struggle with post-traumatic stress following losing three of his mates on the battlefields of Afghanistan. There it was Dan's role and duty to save these mates but he could not. It impacted him profoundly. In addition, in his early years, Dan was far from a model student and was 'invited to leave' his secondary school; sounds to me like code for being 'expelled'. Ben was a self-proclaimed 'fat kid' and a geek. Ben also still claims hand-eye coordination issues. And that is from a guy who ultimately was the commanding officer of the SAS!

From my side: I was badly bullied at school. Moving from Perth as a teenager I landed in an all-boys secondary school where rugby was the only important religion. All-boys schools can be relentlessly cruel and, despite being the school swimming champion, playing first grade Australian Rules football and basketball, to the 'rugby in-group' I was still an outsider. But to my oppressors, what was worse was I challenged their bullying and self-status. They opted to gang together and use derisive comments and physical abuse against me. They publicly called it being 'rejected'. It was coupled with an all too frequent taunt ('*rejecteeeeeed*!'). Being *rejected* lasted around a year. Few other students talked to me for fear that they would be caught up as collateral damage from the rugby-playing cool kids. There were days when I didn't want to go to school. I often felt like crying in the face of the spiteful teasing. My self-esteem was crushed.

But it too did pass. I changed my group of friends to those who were kind and focussed on activities that brought me happiness.

I ignored the bullies until they fell silent. Now, they just seem irrelevant.

A few years ago, I completely ruptured my Achilles tendon. I knew I would be 10 weeks in plaster and not back running for 18 months after rehab. I lay completely dejected on the lounge. Life was over. I was living by myself at the time and thinking about completing simple tasks on crutches was demoralising. But after self-pitying for a short period of time, I decided that there had to be opportunity in this horrendous injury. I made a list of all the things I could do in the gym, then I wrote a gym program to suit. I decided I would also commit to losing a kilogram of body weight a week. I made an appointment to see a nutritionist and had my meals delivered. I started training. My neighbours thought I was going mad as I did intervals on crutches around the block. In an early morning gym session, a guy stopped me mid chin-up. I rested my plaster cast on a bench and took my headphones off. He said to me: *'You know this morning I didn't feel like coming to the gym. But then I thought about you hobbling around training on crutches here for the last two months. And I asked myself, "What's your excuse?"'*

So, yes. All three of us have been beat up, frightened, heartbroken, injured and insulted.

But we aren't making excuses or seeking pity. Neither is Adam. And neither should you.

What's your excuse? Who are you inspiring and how?

We know that life is not fair. It deals you cards that seem unjust. But we would submit to you that there is no happiness without struggle. The cards you have been dealt in this life don't define you. It is your actions that define you. Indeed, to paraphrase the stoic philosopher Epictetus: *We are affected not by events but by the view we take of them.*

There will be many people who doubt you, taunt and bully

you and even ridicule you. When they do, remember the wise words of the Finnish music composer Jan Sibelius.

'Pay no attention to what critics say. There has never been a statue set up to honour a critic.'

We stand with Adam … and with you. Embrace the suck and screw the critics!

Go ahead and build your resilience shield.

Keith Banks is one of many inspirational people in my life. We are pictured together at a Melbourne pub in 2022.

28

Bright with a Chance of Salad

Now that I'm writing the last chapter in my story, I'm taking a moment to reflect. One thing (of the many things) that I have learnt over the past few years is that self-reflection is not narcissistic, it's important.

There was always a reason why I wanted to get these words down on paper. Of course, it was partly for my own self; writing has become a form of therapy for me. I have experienced many emotions during this cathartic experience of self-expression through narrative. Apart from helping myself, I always knew that I wanted to help others. I wanted to tell my story in a way that would start conversations around mental health, which unfortunately, despite the efforts of so many organisations and individuals, still has stigma attached to it. Through telling my story I wanted to be able to encourage others to speak about how they are really feeling and to make changes in their own lives.

I have learnt how truly unstoppable we, as humans, can be. We can push ourselves outside our comfort zones in so many ways. In the past few years, I have undertaken many challenges, some physical, some mental and some emotional, but writing this book has been my greatest challenge and greatest achievement to date.

I now stand up for what is right and what I know to be true. I hope my own story inspires others to stand up for themselves in their pursuit of self-development and self-love. I have fought the black dog and each day I continue to fight it so it doesn't chase me down the road towards Depressionville. It's not an easy fight taming the black dog with its sharp claws and gnashing teeth that will rip you apart if you let it, but Depressionville is not a place that I would want anyone to go to.

I could sit here and rattle off a long list of names of people I want to thank for so many reasons, but most of those people have already been mentioned in this book. They are my tribe and they are my support team. There may not be an 'I' in team, but I am in my team. And so are those very special people who have stuck by me, believed in me and supported me along this journey which has really only just begun.

I wake up every day now thankful that I have another chance. Another chance to feel the sun on my skin (even though I burn easily), another chance to hear the rain on the roof and another chance to breathe the air. These are all things I never used to think about, let alone appreciate.

I know life isn't all roses and I don't always have the time to stop and smell them, but I do now see how beautiful they are as I walk by. I understand that not everything is going to go my way and there will be shit and suffering still to endure. I have learnt that life is not fair. It's not fair for anyone and that's just part of the deal. There are tough times ahead, but the pain and suffering I have already endured has helped to build my resilience shield and to tackle what life throws my way. The mind is a muscle that needs to be worked every day, just like the rest of the body. I now understand that there are going to be good days and there will be bad days but my good days now outweigh the bad ones. Believe me when I say that I used to have more bad days than good, but that was because of the energy I was putting out into the world. It was negative energy. In my opinion everything was shit and so I was getting shit flung back.

A victim mentality is a thing of the past for me. I have a Good2Go mindset. It's a positive mindset that believes that anything is possible. The word impossible means 'I'm possible' and our only limitations are the limitations we put on ourselves. I have crossed paths with so many people who have inspired me to be brave and to be true. They have coached me, pushed me and at times been downright hard on me, but being hard for my own good was what was needed.

For so long, I hid behind my excuses and my 'poor me' attitude. I used to cry out to God saying, 'God, if you exist then why do you let this happen to me? Why am I fat? Why do I have disabilities? Why do I have red hair?' I couldn't find anyone to blame except a higher power and possibly my parents. Blaming, though, wasn't accepting who I was. I was fat, I did have disabilities and yes, I was a ginger. These things weren't God's fault and they certainly were not my parents' fault, they were just what I was. But even after so many years of thinking that I was a victim of some cruel fate, I could still take the reins and change what I could.

My future is looking bright. I have many things on the go and even more things to look forward to. I know why I am here on this earth. It's to share our Australian military history and give veterans a space to tell their own story through my podcast. It's also to start conversations around mental health and help prevent suicides. It's a beautiful thing to work out your purpose, make purposeful decisions and take meaningful steps to achieve what it is you know you want to do.

Change is never easy, but it can be done. I have made huge changes in my mental health, my physical health, how I look, what I eat and drink, what I consume through TV and the media and how I speak and relate to others. I have removed toxins and toxic people from my life. I've allowed myself to be open to professional advice and knowledge, to new ways of thinking and different views. Hell, I even now light candles, put on calming music and wear my cross around my neck. No, I never did join a cult but I did become a leader. The leader of my own life. I took charge and stepped out of the shadows of my old self. I made much needed reforms and changed my life. Now, I order salads for lunch. Yes, I'm still Adam, but I'm not the same easy target any longer, I'm Adam reborn twice.

The 2023 Husky Triathlon was an opportunity to catch up with valued friends and mentors Brooke Strahan (R) and Sarah Watson (L)

MY TEN TOP TIPS

Lessons Learnt During My Journey

The lessons I have learnt during my journey have been many. I do my best to not forget these important lessons and to implement them in my daily life to maintain a positive mindset.

Here are the top ten lessons broken down for you to use and implement in your life so that they may have a positive impact and help you as they have helped me. You always have the power to change your outcomes in life and it must start with you. You alone have to want to make the change. It's got to come from within.

When you embrace the uncomfortable and get comfortable with being uncomfortable, amazing things happen.

1. Control your fear

Fear is an unpleasant emotion caused by the threat of danger, pain or harm. It is completely natural to feel fear; however, if we do not control our fear, it will control us. It's easy to get caught up with fearful thoughts like, 'I'm scared about what people will think of me' or 'What if it doesn't work out?' Fear of others, fear of the unknown. These thoughts can be debilitating and can literally stop you from doing things or achieving goals that your heart desires.

You must be willing to take stock of your fears.

2. Embrace the learning of failure

If you don't fail then you are probably not even trying. With every failure we can grow as a person. Don't accept failure but understand that you may fail and that's a part of the process in real learning. Fall down seven times and get up eight times.

A winner is someone who tried one more time than a loser.

3. Be committed and be consistent

Without commitment you will never start, but, more importantly, without consistency you will never finish. Keep working, keep striving and dream big. Ease is a greater threat to progress than hardship. Keep moving and keep growing. Stay consistent even on the days that you don't want to get up and grind. It is important on those days to turn up and commit to the day.

Commitment doesn't know that it's Sunday.

4. Never stop learning

One of the biggest lessons I've learnt is to keep on learning. Be open to new things and new ways of thinking. Read books, listen to podcasts and don't shut yourself off to those who are different to what you are used to.

If you want to live a life full of abundance then you have to educate yourself.

Learn, do and repeat. Apply lesson number three, stay committed and consistent to being a lifelong learner.

5. Build a support team

To perform at our optimum level, we need the support of a great team. It is very hard to tackle problems on your own. When we collaborate with others we can unlock new ways of thinking and have a new set of eyes on things.

A good team of people around you will help you up when you are down.

The right team will want to see you succeed and they will encourage you to keep striving and chase your dreams.

6. Being mindful of mindfulness

Learning to be mindful has been a real game changer for me. I am now very much aware of how my mind is feeling. If you are not feeling OK, speak up and ask for help. Throughout my journey I have reached out and asked for help at times, because I understood where my mind was at and that asking for help was what was needed. Being in tune with my mind helps me perform at my optimum level. Every day I commit ten minutes to mindfulness before I get up and face the world. I allow myself some time to be with my own thoughts and put my subconscious mind into a positive mode of thinking. I send out positive intentions to the universe. I repeat this practice at night.

Mindfulness leads to a positive mindset and the feeling of being grateful.

7. Be prepared to change your habits

On average, it takes more than two months before a new behaviour becomes automatic — 66 days to be exact. And how long it takes a new habit to form can vary widely depending on the behaviour, the person, and the circumstances. In a study by Dr Phillippa Lally, a UK academic who researches habits, it takes anywhere from 18 days to 254 days for people to form a new habit.[2]

You can't change without forming new habits.

To form a new habit, you have to enforce the new habit and build it into your life. It has to become part of your day, every day. When you want to improve your physical fitness you have to form a habit to train. You may want to run a certain distance, but you may first have to start walking every day, then progress to a light jog every day, then build up the distance and speed day by day. The key is training every day until you form a new habit.

8. You are your environment

There is an old saying that 'if you hang around a barber shop long enough you are going to get a haircut'. This saying highlights how your environment can impact your behaviour and influence your mindset. This can be a good thing or a bad thing depending on your environment. 'If you are hanging around five millionaires you will become the sixth.' I love that saying as it really reinforces how having positivity around you can assist with positive changes in your life. Be aware of your environment and who you are surrounded by.

---

2 *How are habits formed: Modelling habit formation in the real world* by Phillippa Lally first published 16 July 2009.

Our surroundings can influence whether we succeed or fail in life.

So, choose your environment wisely.

9. Allow yourself to dream

One of the biggest changes in my mindset was letting myself dream again. I now dream that anything is possible. Nothing is out of my reach. If you have a dream, then chase that dream and don't let anyone say you can't achieve it. To others, your dream might sound out there and unachievable, but that doesn't mean it is. Just because they can't imagine it being achieved does not mean it can't be. I've said it a few times in this book, but it's so true, 'Before you can achieve, you must believe.'

Protect your dream and don't let others rip it out of your grasp with their words and non-beliefs. If you have the desire to chase a dream, you will achieve it. It may not be achieved quickly, and it may take a lot of work and setbacks, but if you keep working towards it and not give up, you will achieve your dream.

We all have the power to dream because we all have the power to change. It comes down to how much you really want to chase the dream and how willing are you to hold onto that dream when the times are tough. Will you be willing to stay up late and work towards the dream? Are you willing to get up early and do the things you don't want to do but are needed to make the dream come to fruition?

Chasing a dream is not easy, but it can be amazing how far having a dream can take you.

10. Keeping the faith

Faith is one of the most important parts of my personal journey. Understanding that God always has a plan and that he is there for me has not just been a game changer but also an eye opener in my life. Accepting that God does not make mistakes has made me ask God, 'What is it that you know about me that I don't yet know?'

Faith, whether it be in God or just some type of higher power, will see you through the tough times when you think you can't make it. I have learnt to hold the faith.

God's timing is not my timing.
God's timing is perfect.

My faith has helped me along on this journey, because I know that I am never walking alone and that the universe understands me. My faith has helped me write this book. My faith in something bigger than myself has deepened my own faith in myself and what I am capable of. I know that God has great plans for me. I may not always understand the path, but I keep the faith, remembering that God does not make mistakes.

FINAL THOUGHT

Making that phone call on the edge of the cliff has been my greatest success.

It was a pivotal moment. Life is the most important gift that we are given. Ageing is a privilege. Each person's road that they travel on is different, but it's always the journey that is important, not the destination. Because in the end all our destinations are the same.

My journey is only just beginning. I am 31 years old and I still have a lot of living to do. I have a lot of learning to do and I have a lot of loving, laughing and giving back to do.

The world is my oyster and it is your oyster too. Go out and step into your spotlight and when the time is right, be ready to shine and share your own brilliance

... our only limitation is the one we have in our own minds.

Adam Blum

ACKNOWLEDGEMENTS TO MY TRIBE

There are so many people to thank for helping me to tell my story.

To the team at Big Sky Publishing including Denny, Allison, Sharon and Pat, my appreciation for your belief in *Easy Target* and publishing this book. Thank you from the bottom of my heart for allowing me to help others and for stepping me through the publication process.

Janine, you told me I needed to tell my story in a form of a book and I looked at you like you were crazy for proposing such a daunting task. I swiftly said, 'I can't do that'. Despite my response, you believed in me and kept pushing me to write. Eighteen months on, it is now complete, thank you.

Mark, thank you for writing the foreword for me. You are someone I truly respect, my brother, and you have become a true friend. I'm grateful you are in my life.

Johanna, Amelia and Deb, thank you for taking the time out of your busy lives to read my story and write your testimonials. You are an inspiration to me. You don't know how much it means to have you back my story. Thank you from the bottom of my heart.

Paul, Damien, Chris, Hugo, Casey and Sarah, my gratitude to you all for reading *Easy Target* and writing your testimonials. Thank you for your service to our country and everything you do for veterans, the first responders' community and people who are struggling with mental health.

Bec, Keith, Julie, Brooke, Leila, Tim, Dan and Ben, thank you all for believing in my story and sharing your stories in my book to help others. You are all inspirational and I'm grateful to call you my friends.

Brooke, where do I start? Who would have thought that when we first met you would come on this writing journey with me? From that first phone call about possible artwork for the book, then to you coming on board as ghost writer, this book was made possible with your skill, mentoring and encouragement, thank you.

Donna, you said to me all those years ago that I should write a book, so thank you for helping me make that dream a reality.

To Leila from Constant Reader, my gratitude for your help to polish this book with your proofreading and editing. Likewise, Nathan, Pennie and Cameron, thank you for your guidance and advice throughout the whole writing process.

Adam, my brother, you have been such a springboard with *Easy Target* and have helped shape it into what it is now. You have had my back from day one and your friendship is greatly appreciated.

Jo, your mentorship has helped me more than I ever imagined. You have pushed me further than I thought possible, you unlocked the power within and believed in me when I didn't believe in myself. This is only the beginning of great things to come. I am grateful that you are a part of my life.

Sarah, my gratitude for your guidance in helping me as my fitness coach – I wouldn't be where I'm today without you. You are more than a fitness coach to me – you are a mentor – but more importantly, you have become a close friend and have helped through my struggles with injury. Thank you for giving me my good2go mindset.

Sarah Di Lorenzo, my nutritionist, thank you for always keeping me accountable in my weight loss journey; your support has been greatly appreciated.

Jamie, Kristen and Jackie, you have stuck by me through thick and thin. You have seen me at my worst and at my best and you continued to believe in me when I didn't believe in myself, my endless gratitude.

To all of my friends for their support through the dark times and the good times – Kellie, Lyndsay, Sarah M, Elise, Sonya, Rebecca, Chantelle, Darren, Trev, Slatts, Matty M, Mitch P and Andy M – I am so grateful for all that you do and to have you in my life. It's a privilege to have you in my tribe. The best is yet to come.

Mandy, thank you for always being there for me. You have known me from birth and changed many nappies over the years. Your guidance has helped throughout my life.

The Mountain Boys, Ben, Dylan and Kyle, thank you for the cherished memories I have growing up with you all, and to Mick, I want to thank you for taking my call that fateful day, you saved my life.

Ant, thank you for all you have done and helping me get through the tough time of losing Nick. You have been a rock and I'm grateful to call you brother.

To the late 2nd Commando veteran Nick Hill, thank you

for everything you did for me. Your friendship is something I cherished, and I miss you daily. Till Valhalla, brother. Ride free, Commando for life.

To Mum, Dad, Scott, Pip and my extended family, thank you for inspiring me to be all I can be and for always backing me in whatever goals and dreams I set out to achieve. I am where I am today because of your support, guidance, and love.

Nanna, I know you are here with me in spirit and I'm making you proud by living my life to the fullest and by the values you instilled in me. I know you are with me every day, my guardian angel. I love and miss you.

Lastly, I want to thank all my veteran and first responder brothers and sisters who sacrifice so much so we can enjoy the freedom and safety that we have in Australia. Thank you all for your service. It is an honour to serve alongside you all.

SUPPORT SERVICES

Lifeline:
13 11 14, lifeline.org.au

Suicide Call Back Service:
1300 659 467, suicidecallbackservice.org.au

Beyond Blue:
1300 224 636, beyondblue.org.au

MensLine Australia:
1300 789 978, mensline.org.au

Black Dog Institute:
blackdoginstitute.org.au

More from Big Sky Publishing

Empowering stories of overcoming adversity

Campfire for a Woman's Heart

Stories of Resilience from Inspirational Women

Dr Kirsty Sword Gusmão, AO
Margaret Cunneen, SC
Dr Kay Danes OAM
Liesl Tesch AM and more ...

Natalie Stockdale
With a foreword by Dr Lucy Hone

More from Big Sky Publishing

A book for all those suffering similarly… you will see yourself on every page.

The Inv*s*ble TRAUMA

Coping with PTSD

An honest and hopeful account

DAVE MORGAN

View sample pages, reviews and information on this book and other titles at www.bigskypublishing.com.au

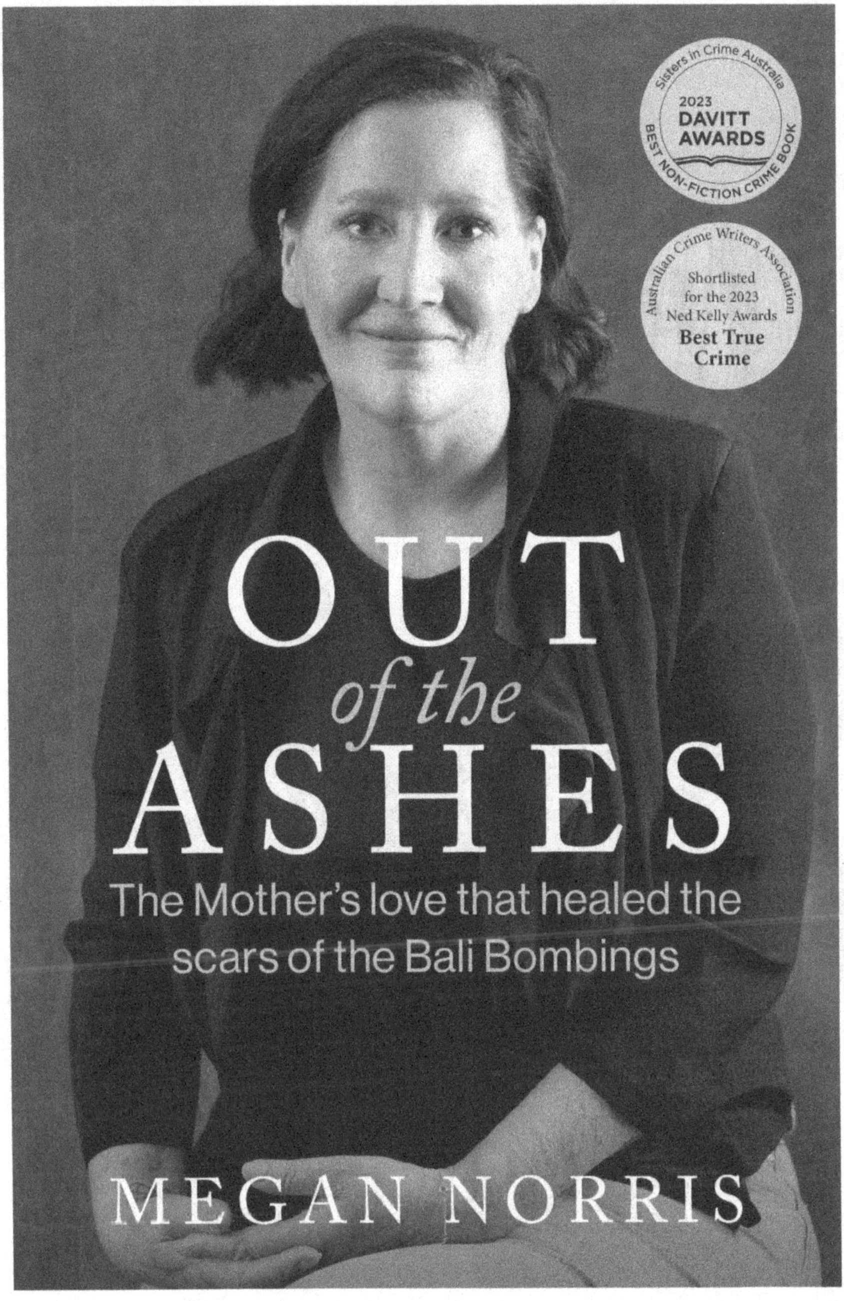

More from Big Sky Publishing

DRUNK ON

Confidence

UNAPOLOGETICALLY ME...
FROM LOST & ANXIOUS TO
SELF-ASSURED.

A memoir

HEIDI ANDERSON

View sample pages, reviews and information on this book and other titles at
www.bigskypublishing.com.au